Home
Smoking and
Curing

Home Smoking and Curing

HOW TO SMOKE-CURE FISH, MEAT AND GAME

Keith Erlandson

EBURY PRESS
LONDON

First published in 1989 by Century
Hutchinson Ltd. Published in 1993 by
Vermilion, reprinted in 1997 by
Ebury Press.
This revised edition published in 2003
by Ebury Press.

5 7 9 10 8 6 4

This edition first published by
Ebury Press, Random House,
20 Vauxhall Bridge Road, London
SW1V 2SA

Random House Australia Pty Limited,
20 Alfred Street, Milsons Point,
Sydney, New South Wales 2061,
Australia

Random House New Zealand Limited,
18 Poland House, Glenfield,
Auckland 10, New Zealand

Random House
South Africa Pty Limited,
Endulini, 5A Jubilee Road,
Parktown 2193, South Africa

The Random House Group Limited
Reg. No. 954009

www.randomhouse.co.uk

A CIP catalogue for this book is
available from the British Library

ISBN 0091890292

Printed and bound in Great Britain by
Mackays of Chatham plc, Kent

CONTENTS

Introduction

Smoked foods today are much more popular than they were in, say, the immediate years following the Second World War. We live in a high-tech age yet traditional ways of cooking seem to be flourishing. I remember just before the first edition of this book was published an article appeared in one of the more responsible and less sensational Sunday newspapers on Pinney's Smokehouse in Suffolk, which, even then, had been established for several years. More than thirty years on, as this edition goes to press, I came across another article on Pinney's in another Sunday newspaper. The fact that this smokehouse has endured for more than fifty years, and continues to attract attention from the national press, serves as a pointer to the enduring appeal of smoked foods.

The first article, published more than thirty years ago, shared a page with a piece on smoking techniques which could be practised at home. Rudimentary salting procedures were described, together with simple smoking equipment which the average handyman could easily construct, and a few basic smoking recipes were given for food such as salmon, chicken and trout. The information was sketchy and not very accurate, but at least it did make an attempt to put the business of home smoking before the public eye. I had myself been smoke-curing for some time before this article appeared, but this was the first time I had ever seen any mention of the subject in a form which was likely to be read by a large section of the British public. The article then struck me as timely as for some years there had been an awareness, that continues today, of the enjoyment and sense of accomplishment that can be gained from the pursuit of traditional crafts such as home brewing beer and wine, building furniture in one's own workshop and curing and tanning hides, to mention but a few. In all these activities there is a considerable amount of job satisfaction, as the operator ventures into fields hitherto understood only by the masters of the various crafts.

Just as pheasant- and other game-rearing was once considered to be the province of a full-time gamekeeper , the keen amateur has now discovered that he can rear a few dozen or even a few hundred birds in his back garden just as efficiently as his professional counterpart. The same applies to home smoking.

In this age of mass production, some so-called smoked foods have no contact with real smoke but are painted with smoke essence, which I understand is a substance similar to the tar that collects on the interior of a smoking kiln. Good smoked food, when available, is very expensive. In addition, many smoked foods are not available at all in Britain, yet you might be very keen to try some. The answer is to smoke them yourself. High quality raw products are hardly likely to be cheap, yet even though you may pay top market price for fresh salmon, chicken or trout, the home-smoked product will still average out as considerably cheaper than the commercially smoked and marketed product and you will know what all the ingredients are.

Many people in Britain fish for both game and sea fish, others shoot feathered game, and the country now has many dedicated deer stalkers. It is to these people in particular that a comprehensive knowledge of smoke curing can be so useful. In particular it offers alternative ways of eating their catches of fish and bags of game. A surfeit of fresh salmon palls and there are surely limits to the amount of roast or casseroled wildfowl a person would wish to eat.

The commercial smoker must cater for the 'average palate', but we all know full well that, in reality, no such thing as the average palate exists, particularly in the matter of salt and other seasoning. As a home smoker you are in a position to have your product salty or mild, lightly or heavily smoked. You can experiment and vary the process until you get a product exactly to your liking; so, through no fault of the commercial smoker, the home smoker should be able to produce a far more satisfactory product, to his or her own taste, than could be bought in the shops.

It can be very difficult to find reliable information on home smoking, even today. I am indebted to the staff of the Torry Research Station, Aberdeen and the Food and Agricultural Organisation of the United Nations, who published some of the original pamphlets on the smoke curing of fish and the construction of smoke houses. I must stress the need for experimentation and the working out of suitable techniques by trial and error, and freely admit that a skilled operator, using simple traditional equipment, can produce better results than an unskilled or careless person operating a sophisticated mechanical smoker costing many thousands of pounds.

Working on the broad principles of fish smoking, I have evolved my own methods and equipment for the smoking of poultry, meat and game, by the trial and error methods and with (ultimate) complete success. I hope to be able to instruct my readers in the next few chapters to prepare most of the smoked delicacies enjoyed at the moment in other European countries and I believe at the present time may be exclusive in this country to me.

1 The Origins of Smoke Curing

It is impossible to define the precise point when the smoke curing of fish and meat came into being. Possibly it was discovered during the Stone Age, when primitive people used fires to warm themselves and cook their food, having fish or meat hanging in the same cave or shelter as the fire. They may have discovered that the food acquired a distinctive and pleasant flavour through being brought into contact with wood smoke, and that its keeping qualities were considerably enhanced – a most important consideration, as they depended on hunting. There might be times when they would succeed in driving a whole herd of reindeer into a roughly constructed enclosure and a great killing would take place. A mammoth might be taken in a game pit, or a fresh run of salmon could supply them with a great quantity of fish. In all these cases the hunters would have far more food than would be required for their immediate needs, but these early forbears of ours were sufficiently intelligent and far-sighted to realize that some time hence, game might be temporarily scarce or nonexistent, and the salmon run always came to an end eventually. It is therefore perfectly logical to suppose that primitive people had a keen interest in preserving their surplus food against leaner times, when a supply of smoked or dried fish or flesh could spell the difference between survival and oblivion.

Again, it is impossible to define when pre-salting or brining was adopted as an essential part of the process as it is recognized today. It is safe to say that, the higher the salt content in a product and the longer the smoking period employed, the better its keeping qualities will be.

About 40 miles from where I write, on the tidal reaches of Conway, is an ancient stone-built salmon trap. Within a few yards of this trap is a cave, whose mouth is covered at high tide. The interior of the cave rises upwards, above the water level, and according to local legend the Romans used to smoke their salmon in this cave, probably lighting their fire at low tide. The cave mouth would have been sealed by the rising tide, and the salmon were ready by the time the tide receded again.

I think we can safely dismiss the story of the first finnan haddock. It is said that a Scottish fisherman by the name of Finson customarily hung his haddock catches to dry by his barn. One night the barn caught fire and, though most of the catch was ruined, Finson managed to salvage a few of the less damaged ones. These were eaten and enjoyed, and so finnan haddock came into being. To me, this sounds impossible. Intense heat would be generated by the burning barn, enough to cook the fish, even though it would be sufficiently out of reach to escape being burned to a cinder. Finnan haddock require a very gentle smoking process, at a temperature not in excess of 29°C (85°F), otherwise they will cook and disintegrate.

2 Smoked fish and game in Scandinavia

Many years ago my wife and I did an extensive tour of the Scandinavian peninsula, covering a distance of over 4,000 miles. Apart from the cleanliness and very obvious prosperity of the two countries visited (Norway and Sweden), I was particularly impressed by the manner in which the Scandinavians utilize their natural resources of fish and game.

After I landed in Bergen, my first call was to a fishmonger. Old memories of smoked mackerel still lingered, and we secured a supply. When we ate them the following day on the way to Trondheim, we found them oily-skinned and difficult to dismember – very palatable, but not as memory told me they should be. A visit to Trondheim fish market was an education and cleared up the doubts about the mackerel. Everything seemed larger than life. Huge salmon, fresh and smoked, reposed upon the slabs. The lobsters varied from ordinary to gigantic and the halibut were the largest I have seen. Sea bream were much in evidence, split open and rather glutinous in appearance, and there were mackerel, fresh and smoked. There were two types of smoked mackerel – the dark, oily kind we had already sampled and others with wrinkled golden skins, which I realized were the excellent hot-smoked variety, ready to eat, that we wanted. We realized then that the Bergen mackerel were only cold-smoked and needed cooking. We had eaten them raw.

In a Lapland supermarket we purchased fresh grayling and smoked perch. Perch are very highly esteemed in Sweden and are the same price as smoked trout. When I considered the many thousands of perch that must be returned to water annually by coarse fishermen in Britain, I realized we were missing something. My wife and son did not care for the perch but I found them excellent. They were dark, firm and waxy fleshed, with a distinctive, powerful flavour.

At Jokkmok, a former Lapp village, now a small but important town, we purchased some lightly smoked reindeer haunch, which, owing to the mackerel experience, we realized we would have to cook. We fried it at the roadside and found it quite palatable, although we felt we could have improved upon it with more time, knowledge and additives.

Further south, a visit to Stockholm game market proved well worthwhile. The stalls were decorated with elk heads and stuffed goshawks, and, although the game season had not started, there were several specimens from cold store, including a fair quantity of ptarmigan in full winter plumage, all with their feet removed (grouse claw brooches?). These were accompanied by a rather weary-looking hen capercaillie and three even more unappetising mallard, priced at what was then a rather expensive £1.55 each. Even more extortionate were oven-ready wood pigeon at 70p each. I was asked £8.50 for an entire haunch of smoked roe but settled for just a kilo. This was hot-smoked and ready to eat, and was quite delicious. We also saw smoked badger hams, pike, huge smoked eels and masses of freshwater crayfish.

Back in my own province of Bohuslan, on the west coast, we looked up the daughter of a famous local hunter, whom I knew 36 years previously. His main quarry had been roe, elk and willow grouse, which he shot over an English setter. This lady was able to fill me in on how an elk is dealt with. A young elk will provide excellent steaks but what, I asked, does one do with an old bull as big as a Shire horse? They are best made into meatballs. Being dry fleshed, it is better mixed with pork in equal quantities. I do know that BB shot works out at 70 pellets to the ounce. How many meatballs to an elk?

While on the west coast, we took a day trip to Oslo, mainly to see the Viking ships. However, I found a fishmonger offering the only cheap food of the whole tour – grayling. They were large fish, running three to a kilo, and my wife cooked them using a trout recipe. Nothing could have been better. They were entirely different in character from a Welsh grayling: deeper and fatter, more silvery and with tiny mouths. In flavour they were the equal of any salmon. Our local ones taste like the bed of the Dee.

We found so many good things to eat on our trip, particularly of the smoked variety, which are either completely unobtainable in this country or can only be found at considerable trouble and expense, that we decided to develop our own smoking techniques, using simple, traditional methods as practised by the Lapps, Red Indians and the small Scottish salmon curers.

3 The basic smoking process

I think at this point we might consider exactly what modern smoking processes consist of.

SALTING

Before smoking commences, the raw materials are either dry-salted or soaked in brine. The salt helps to preserve the product but this is less important nowadays, thanks to modern storage and refrigeration techniques. It is not so much to preserve food that smoking is employed in the Western hemisphere now as to give it a pleasant and distinctive flavour, the salt acting more as a seasoning than a preservative. These remarks do not, however, apply to hot countries like Africa and the Far East, where the preservation of the catch is of the utmost importance.

HUMIDITY AND WEIGHT LOSS

During the smoking process, tarry deposits from the smoke settle on the product. These deposits are of an antiseptic nature and, along with the salt already absorbed, tend to inhibit the development of the spoilage bacteria, which, left to their own devices, cause fish or flesh to putrify. During smoking, weight loss occurs in the product, due to evaporation of moisture from within the tissues. This evaporation and subsequent weight loss are absolutely essential to successful smoking, and it follows that the greater the weight loss, the greater the keeping qualities. The weight loss is directly linked to the humidity of the atmosphere prevailing at the time of smoking, so that in a traditional kiln a side of salmon or a fillet of beef will take longer to dry out sufficiently under humid conditions than under relatively dry ones. In the modern mechanical kiln, humidity is controlled automatically, so these variations in smoking times do not occur, but the home smoker using traditional methods must always be aware of this factor and be prepared to allow for it accordingly.

There are two methods of smoking employed in European countries: cold- and hot-smoking.

COLD-SMOKING

Cold-smoking smokes but does not cook the product. It is usually done at temperatures between 10 and 29°C (50 and 85°F), ideally, 24–26°C (75–80°F). Cold-smoking temperatures are, to a certain extent, governed by the temperature outside. Where ambient temperatures are low, it is quite possible to smoke successfully at far lower temperatures than available literature suggests is possible, provided one is prepared to spend more time on the process. At a time of high ambient temperatures, it is important that smoking temperatures are kept sufficiently low in the case of fish, or the product will cook and disintegrate. Some cold-smoked products are eaten raw, e.g. salmon, cod's roe and beef fillet, whereas others, such as finnan haddock, kippers and cod fillets, require a further period of cooking in the kitchen.

HOT-SMOKING

After dry-salting or brining, hot-smoked products are first cold-smoked for varying periods to dry them out partially and to impart a smoked flavour. In the case of fish, the temperature is then raised to about 82°C (180°F) – never more than 93°C (200°F) – and the fish are cooked for a time in the hot smoke. Care must be taken during the initial cold-smoking that temperatures do not exceed 29°C (85°F) or the fish will case harden, preventing further smoke penetration or adequate loss of moisture.

Meat, poultry and game are easier to hot-smoke than fish. Care must be exercised during their cold-smoking periods to avoid case hardening, as with fish, and for exactly the same reasons. However, during their hot-smoking periods these meats are far more tolerant of variations in temperature, and a range of 82–115°C (180–240°F) might be suitable for the same product, though a batch of fish would be ruined in the higher temperature ranges. Nevertheless, even these relatively tolerant products can be spoilt by excessive temperatures or overcooking. Apart from becoming unacceptably dry in texture, the product tends to lose its smoky character, so an overdone haunch of venison will simply resemble dry roast meat.

Once the basic principles are mastered and, in particular, the correct salt content, it is surprising just how cheap and easy it is to manufacture really first-class smoked products.

4 The raw material

FISH

There is some debate about the quality of farmed fish. I have had no problems when smoking farmed trout but farmed salmon is different. Most farmed salmon have no muscle tone, as the fish don't live a natural life where they have to battle against currents. The flesh is flaccid and won't hang up, so it must be smoked flat. Personally I would always prefer to smoke wild salmon than farmed.

In some quarters there is a completely erroneous belief that stale fish can be used for smoking, as the smoking process will impart its own flavour to the fish and thus mask any defects in quality. Certainly it is just possible to 'save the life' of stale fish by smoking, so that it is just edible, but, at the best, only a very inferior product both in keeping quality and flavour can result.

Fish that is to be smoked must be completely fresh to obtain the best results, although this is a good point at which to dispel the belief that frozen goods are not suitable for smoking. This is completely untrue. All frozen fish (and game, meat and poultry) can be employed, and first-class results obtained, as long as the fish was frozen as soon as it was caught.

However, in the case of salmon, a better-looking finished product can be obtained from fresh fish. This is because the moisture between the fibres turns to ice within the fish during freezing. When the fish is allowed to thaw out, prior to smoking, this water runs away, taking some of the fish's natural oil with it. However carefully the fish is filleted, some gaps will appear between the fibres of the cut surface, causing a more unsightly finish than if the cut surface could be kept smooth and unblemished. Frozen salmon is altogether more tender to handle when thawed out than the fresh fish.

FAT CONTENT

This mention of the oil loss suffered by thawed-out salmon brings one to the connection between the relative fat content of all raw products to be smoked and the salt content they are required to absorb during pre-salting or brining. Anything with a high fat content is more resistant to salt penetration than anything with a lower concentration of fat. It follows, therefore, that a fat, fresh-run salmon will require longer in the brine than a fish of equal size that has been hanging about a river during a period of low water, or alternatively, has come many miles inland, negotiating scores of obstacles on the way. I was told a story of a Scottish salmon smoker who attended to the needs of several fishermen who fished the length of a famous salmon river. At one period when he was extremely busy and his kiln was full to capacity, a friend called in and was shown fish from practically every beat on the river. Even to an unpractised eye, it was apparent that the best-conditioned fish came from the lower reaches of the river, while the higher up the river the fish had been caught, the thinner they became.

There are no hard and fast rules to apply to this question of differing fat content. One must play it by ear and use intelligent guesswork. If I am brining a batch of pheasants and I notice one is lacking in fat under the skin, it comes out of the brine 15 minutes before the others; if I am preparing fillets of beef and some have that marbling of fat between the tissues, visible at the sliced ends and the hallmark of superbly conditioned cattle, they receive 30 minutes longer in the brine than the very lean, solid red fillets.

MEAT

Whereas fish for smoking must be as fresh as possible, which should present no problem to the home smoker who smokes his or her own fresh catches, other products require a different approach. Beef will not absorb salt unless it has been hanging for a minimum of one week, and 10 days to a fortnight is better. It is essential to know and trust one's butcher. So many modern butchers do not hang their meat for long enough before selling, but there are still some old-fashioned rural butchers who do. Ideally, the beef should hang in the carcase, but if only fresh fillets can be obtained they can be 'aged' in a refrigerator (not a freezer). They will probably become a little tainted when ageing in a refrigerator, but a wash in vinegar solution before brining will take care of this problem. No meat or game should be allowed to become really high before smoking, as a gamy taste conflicts with the smoky flavour. Venison should hang for one week to 10 days. Pheasant, grouse, mallard, duck, geese, turkey and chicken are best done fairly fresh, 3 days dead being ideal. I have smoked thousands of quail that have been frozen within 24 hours of killing, and this appears to be perfectly satisfactory.

FREEZER STORAGE

If you are going to store foods in the freezer before smoking them, all ageing must be done when they are in their fresh condition, and they must be processed immediately upon thawing out.

Salmon should be frozen with their heads on and guts intact. As they do not feed in fresh water, their innards are empty, so gut tainting does not result. Trout should be gutted and the blood channel along the spine scraped out before freezing. Eel guts taint very rapidly, so they should be gutted as soon as possible, but the chief secret of successful eel smoking is the removal of the kidney. The eel has one kidney, buried deep in the flesh – 4 cm (1½ inches) below the vent. You must slice into this area and scrape out the kidney, for if it is left within the eel it will make the finished product unpalatable.

All poultry and winged game should be plucked and drawn prior to freezing. I once froze a batch of pheasants intact but they suffered a certain degree of gut tainting. They were still quite palatable but, knowing their history as I did, I could just detect a degree of tainting, although others did not.

If you intend to store anything in the freezer for any length of time, it is an excellent idea to wrap it in aluminium foil or brown paper, which will protect it from freezer burn and subsequent dehydration to a far greater degree than polythene freezer bags.

5   Pre-salting

As I have already mentioned, the addition of salt to the raw material is an essential part of the smoke-curing process. The product is either completely covered in dry salt for a period or soaked in brine of varying strengths according to what is being processed.

Dry-salting is favoured by commercial fish smoking concerns, particularly in the case of salmon, as the dry salt attracts moisture from the tissues of the fish, causing a weight loss of up to 9% during this part of the process. It follows, therefore, that the time the fish will need in the smoking kiln will be much reduced, as about half the weight loss required in the finished product will already have taken place. So the whole process can be speeded up, and of course in any commercial enterprise time means money. To home smokers, speeding up the process is not important, as in any case they will be conducting the operation partly as a hobby. I have no hesitation, therefore, in recommending the use of brine as opposed to dry salt (but see 'Dry-salting and other methods' on page 29).

BRINING

In common with all minority activities of a traditional nature, there are a number of closely guarded 'secrets' connected with smoke curing. So it is with brining. In bygone days, secret ingredients were added to the brines: brown sugar, molasses, rum, white pepper, saltpetre, cloves and bay leaves, all of which were alleged to impart additional flavour to smoked salmon. Yet all that is required to make a first-class smoked product is pure vacuum-dried salt, which is very cheap.

Originally, wooden brining tubs were employed. Metal should be avoided, as it can taint the product. Modern plastic vessels are particularly suitable, and a plastic dustbin is ideal. Crockery or earthenware vessels can also be used for brining small quantities of food.

As the home smoker is unlikely to be dealing with large quantities of food at any one time, there is no reason why you should not use a fresh lot of brine for everything you process. This is far more hygienic than keeping used brine and adding more salt to it in order to keep the strength up to the required level, as bacteria can breed in stale brine.

In large smoking plants, it is customary to use the same lot of brine for several batches of fish, adding more salt and checking the concentration of the brine by floating a salinometer in the liquid. This instrument gives a reading of the salt concentration. The raw product absorbs salt from the brine solution, causing it to become weaker, hence the need to add more solid salt. The most widely used brine is an 80% solution, which is formed by dissolving 1.2 kg (2 lb 10¼ oz) of salt in each 4.54 litres (1 gallon) of water. Make the solution by adding the salt to 1.7 litres (3 pints) of hot or boiling water, giving it a good stir to dissolve the salt partly, then adding another 2.84 litres (5 pints) of cold water and stirring again. As some products require different brine strengths, a table is given in Appendix 2.

When brining, it is not a good idea to pack the fish or other articles too closely together, otherwise the brine may be denied access to all parts. As they will float to the surface, they must be weighted down, so that they remain at all times completely submerged. A good idea is to place a wire cake cooling rack on the surface, with a fairly heavy object such as a 3 kg (7 lb) weight on top of the rack. A 2.25 litre (4 pint) plastic ice-cream box partially filled with water also makes a convenient weight. During the brining period, it is advisable to lift the weight once or twice and agitate the contents. After the brine has been used, it can be re-used as a good non-selective weed-killer, particularly on waste ground or garden paths. Brining tubs should always be well washed after use.

Fish should be brined separately from meat, poultry or game, or these other products will become fish-tainted. There is, however, no objection to their sharing the same smoking kiln later on.

Strong and weak brines

My own preference is for a fairly strong brine (80–90%), in which the fish, fowl or flesh is left for a matter of hours rather than days, but there is an alternative method involving the use of weaker brines, plus sugar and in some cases other ingredients. The material is left in these weaker brines often for a period of several days. Although it is not usual to brine fish in this manner, the method has a definite place in the curing of certain meats and fowl which, owing to their age or species, are likely to be very tough.

Salt has a hardening effect upon the muscular tissue of mammalian and avian flesh, but sugar tenderizes, so a tough bird such as an aged goose, pheasant or turkey could benefit from treatment in sugar-added brine. However, where the method really comes into its own is when you have to deal with a piece of less than prime-quality beef or a joint of elderly bear, elk or wild boar. The British home smoker is hardly likely to be faced with any of these last three commodities. Even if you have friends in the USA or Scandinavia who might conceivably send you some of these meats, the Department for the Environment, Food and Rural Affairs would hardly be kindly disposed to their importation. Nevertheless, the method could prove very useful when brining venison from an old stag, and it is also customary to use this so-called 'sweet pickle' brining method when curing bacon or ham, either smoked or unsmoked. When strong brines are employed for a few hours, the temperature of the brine is of little consequence as the food does not remain in the pickle for any length of time, but when using the longer 'sweet pickle' brining process certain procedures must be observed. When a lengthy brining process is involved, the pickle should first be chilled to about 1.5°C (35°F) before the meat is immersed. Throughout the entire length of the cure, the liquid must be maintained at this temperature by refrigeration to prevent spoilage. However, if you notice that the brine is beginning to smell sour, pour it away at once and wash the meat in a weak vinegar solution. The vessel should be washed out and scalded and a fresh batch of pickle made.

Whether you use the short, strong brining process or the longer one involving sweet pickle, the contents of the brining vessel should be agitated from time to time. Brine weakens towards the surface, so the agitation will ensure that the brine remains at a more consistent strength; when brining in sweet pickle for several days, it is a good idea to turn the meat or birds over daily.

Sweet pickle
38.6 litres (8½ gallons) water
2.25 kg (5 lb) vacuum-dried salt
450 g (1 lb) white sugar
28 g (1 oz) saltpetre
112 g (4 oz) pickling spice

Brine for octopus or squid
29.5 litres (6½ gallons) water
295 g (10½ oz) salt
900 g (2 lb) brown sugar
1.75 litres (62 fl oz) soy sauce
3 cups lemon juice
4 tablespoons garlic juice (if available)
4 tablespoons onion juice (if available)
6 tablespoons ground ginger

Vacuum-dried salt can be purchased from most agricultural merchants, and if you scan the yellow pages of your telephone directory an entry under 'Salt merchants' will usually be discovered. Salt attracts atmospheric moisture, so it is worth paying a little more for salt packed in a stout plastic sack than a paper one. It is best stored in a closed container such as a plastic domestic dustbin with a well-fitting lid. If salt does become damp and lumpy it will still be fit to use, but bulk for bulk will weigh a little heavier than dry salt, owing to the moisture it has absorbed. If using damp salt, 55–85 g (2–3 oz) more per 4.54

litres (1 gallon) of water should be used than recommended in the tables.

Saltpetre

Saltpetre (sodium nitrate) is added to some cures for meat and fish because it helps to preserve the colour and inhibits the growth of harmful bacteria. Because it is classed as a dangerous substance, it is available from pharmacists only and has to be ordered in advance. Store it in an airtight jar, clearly labelled, in a safe place.

The brining pump

Brine has a very penetrative effect upon the tissues of fish and flesh. The salt content of the brine blends with the fluid content of the meat or fish and works its way through the tissues towards the interior. However, when very thick pieces of meat or very large birds are being processed, there may be such a depth of flesh that it is difficult for the brine to penetrate right to the interior. An aid to effective penetration is the brine pump, which works on exactly the same principle as the hypodermic syringe, except that the brine is forced out of holes in the side of the needle instead of the tip.

The greatest advantage of the brining pump is that it can be plunged in close to the bone of hams and large haunches of venison, as it is around the bones where a type of deterioration called 'bone tainting' can arise.

If the pump has been out of action for some time, the plunger should be soaked in water for 3 hours to soften and expand it. Before filling, the needle should be sterilized by holding it under boiling water for 20 seconds. The needle should be dipped into

BRINE PUMP

the brine until its entire length is covered, then the plunger should be fully withdrawn and the cylinder of the syringe is filled. The needle should be driven into the flesh at an angle, right to the bone, but the full charge of brine should not be deposited at this point. As the plunger is depressed, the needle should be slowly drawn out and will distribute brine around its path to the surface. When the needle is withdrawn, the tissues around the exit hole should be firmly pressed with the fingers to prevent the brine leaking out.

It is most important that the pump should be kept scrupulously clean, otherwise bacteria as well as brine may be injected into the meat. About 30 ml (1 fl oz) per 450 g (1 lb) of meat should be injected. The meat should then be immersed in brine for the usual period, to ensure maximum distribution of brine throughout the tissues. The brine pump should be used as a piece of auxiliary equipment, not as an end in itself. After use, the pump should be dismantled, then thoroughly washed and dried before it is put away.

DRY-SALTING AND OTHER METHODS

In addition to the strong brines that I favour for use in most of my own smoking and curing operations, and the sweet pickle brine already described for use during other processes, I will also outline alternative brining methods and seasoning techniques, plus dry-salting methods for fish curing. You may prefer these, since dry-salting removes more water from the fish during the curing process than does brining. The smoking process can then be shortened, as the fish only needs to make half the total required weight loss during actual smoking, since the other half has already been lost during dry-salting.

To dry-salt fish, either filleted or split, a bed of either plain vacuum-dried salt or special dry cure, (see below), should be made about 2.5 cm (1 inch) thick on a wooden or plastic surface. When several fish are to be dry-salted, a stack of fish should be formed by laying a split fish, or two fillets side by side, skin-side down on the bed of salt. The cut surfaces should be covered with a 1.2 cm (½ inch) layer of salt over the thickest parts of the fish, thinning to a mere sprinkling towards the thinnest parts of the tails. Another split fish or pair of fillets is then placed on top of this layer of salt, skin-side down, and the process repeated until the stack is complete, the last layer of fish being covered with a 1.2 cm (½ inch) layer of salt or dry cure, with the exception of the tail. The salting time varies according to size, fat content and species of fish involved. Small salmon fillets (670–900 g/1½–2 lb) require about 5–6 hours. Medium fillets (1.34–1.8 kg/3–4 lb) require 8–9 hours, while fillets of 2.25 kg (5 lb) and upwards will require 12–14 hours. Note that, in the case of split fish, double the weight of a certain-sized fillet only requires salting for the same length of time as quoted for a single fillet. During the salting process, brine will be formed, as water is extracted from the fish and drains away from the stack of fish. After salting, the fish should be well washed in cold water to remove all traces of surface salt, then soaked in fresh water for 5 minutes and hung up to dry for 24 hours. In the case of non-fatty fish such as cod or haddock, salting times should be decreased by 25%.

Dry cure for fish
3.58 kg (8 lb) salt
1.8 kg (4 lb) brown sugar
55 g (2 oz) saltpetre
4 tablespoons white pepper
2 tablespoons garlic powder (if available)

Special dry cure for fish
3.58 kg (8 lb) salt
1.8 kg (4 lb) brown sugar
55 g (2 oz) saltpetre
6 tablespoons garlic powder (if available)
6 tablespoons crushed cloves
6 tablespoons onion powder (if available)
6 tablespoons crushed bay leaves
6 tablespoons crushed mace

PRE-DRYING

With the exception of trout and eels, which are placed in the smoker when wet with brine, most products will benefit from a pre-drying period before being placed in the smoker. This will get rid of any excess moisture and will reduce the smoking period required accordingly. It is recommended that salmon sides should hang in a room at about 21°C (70°F) for 24 hours prior to smoking, or at least overnight. Poultry, venison, game and beef should hang for the same period, but small birds such as quail, grouse and woodcock only need to pre-dry for about 3

31

hours. Of course the relative humidity of the atmosphere will have some bearing on the required pre-drying period, so one must again 'play it by ear'. It is rather important that small birds, pheasants, venison, beef and fish should be protected from a drying wind when pre-drying, otherwise they will case harden, with the same results as if over-rapid smoke drying was allowed to take place (domestic ducks would not be similarly affected, owing to the very oily nature of their skins).

6 Fuels

WOOD FOR SMOKE PRODUCTION

The essential commodity upon which the success of any smoke-curing operation depends is a suitable supply of smoke-producing fuel. What is required is a fuel that will burn slowly and steadily, requiring the minimum of attention, and without producing too much heat. Non-resinous woods must be used, as resinous softwoods impart a bitter flavour to the food, although giving it an attractive colour. Some people mix a proportion of softwood sawdust with that of the hardwood variety, which they claim adds colour without impairing the flavour of the smoked product.

Basically, any British hardwood can be used for smoke production. Oak is traditional but beech, ash, elm, sycamore and hickory are all perfectly suitable, or any mixture of these. The Lapps use birch almost exclusively, with, I suspect, some alder. Spanish oak must be avoided as it gives the food a rather unpleasant antiseptic flavour. Sawdust, chips or small logs of all these woods can be used, but if fires of solid fuel are made, they will require regular attention. At times they will flare up and cook the product, if not restrained. At other times they will die down and need replenishing. The most consistent fuel of all is sawdust. It does not flare into life but smoulders with a steady glow for hours on end, producing a fairly consistent column of smoke: 1½–2 biscuit-tinfuls of oak sawdust will, if placed in a suitable receptacle, burn without attention for 12–15 hours. Having stated that sawdust is my preference, I will say that branches of juniper or gorse can be added to the final stages of salmon smoking; they are aromatic but non-resinous woods and can add a distinctive flavour to the salmon.

Sources of supply

There now arises the essential question of where to find a supply of the fuel of your choice. At most sawmills, the sawdust from all operations goes into a large collective sump. In addition to the essential British hardwoods, the sump will in all probability contain sawdust of pine, larch and spruce, in addition to those of foreign timbers such as mahogany, teak and iroku. This conglomerate mixture is quite unsuitable for smoking. Look for small, rural sawmills, particularly in stock-raising areas where there is a steady demand for hardwood stock-fencing stakes. These stakes are trimmed and pointed individually at a sawbench; consequently the sawdust from them is unadulterated by unsuitable timbers, and sackfuls can usually be reserved for the smoker by a co-operative foreman.

HOT-SMOKING FUELS

In addition to smoke-producing fuel, the smoker will also require a fuel to produce sufficient heat for hot-smoking various products. Although small logs will provide sufficient heat, these fires are difficult to control to the correct temperatures, so in all my own hot-smoking operations I use Calor gas and gas rings. How, I will explain later. I see no reason why electrical elements should not be incorporated in a hot-smoker by any handyman competent in these matters, but being one of those persons with such a horror of electricity that I don rubber boots and gloves to change a torch battery, I will leave such ventures to those more knowledgeable.

In addition to the hardwoods already mentioned, hedgerow woods such as hawthorn and blackthorn can be used. Apple, pear, plum and damson are all excellent, and have the added advantage of imparting a particularly pleasant flavour to the product. However, as these woods are not sawn commercially but are normally used as fuel only in rural areas, it will hardly be possible to obtain them in the convenient form of sawdust or chips. Thinly cut slices of these woods can, however, be cut with a chain saw, and large logs from mature fruit trees can be split with an axe to produce conveniently sized and readily combustible pieces. To prevent these solid fuels bursting into flame and producing excessive heat, the wood should be kept damp, but a disadvantage of this practice is that damp fuel produces smoke that is heavily moisture-laden. The product receiving attention will take far longer to dry out under these circumstances, consequently prolonging the process. This situation can be avoided by using dry sand to damp down the fire burning solid fuel.

At one time, a salmon smoker pursued his craft in a particularly treeless area in the west of Ireland, where the supply of fresh salmon was excellent but the supply of fuel was restricted to peat. On being asked how he managed to find a supply of suitable smoke-producing fuel in such a timberless land, this worthy gentleman revealed that he had a working arrangement with the local undertaker, who imported oak and other hardwood boards for the manufacture of coffins, so was able to keep the salmon smoker supplied with wood chips and offcuts, all dry and nicely seasoned.

Another acquaintance of mine lived in South Africa for a time and was fond of smoking mackerel and snoek, which he caught in considerable numbers off Capetown. His smoking kiln consisted of a derelict upright-type refrigerator with part of the top cut away. His fuel was obtained from the local brewery, which apparently manufactured its own oak barrels and was able to supply my friend with chips, shavings and offcuts in the same manner that the undertaker supplied the Irishman. So if you have difficulty at first in finding suitable fuels, you would be well advised to consider whether there are any local industries in your particular district that could keep you supplied.

7 Equipment

THE TRADITIONAL COLD-SMOKER

Cold-smoking, at temperatures of around 26°C (80°F), is an essential operation for the production of smoked salmon, which is eaten raw, of other smoked fish, such as kippers, finnan haddock, cod and haddock fillets and cod roes, and fillets of beef. Cold-smoking is also an essential part of the initial processing of all products that are ultimately hot-smoked.

In the commercial fish-smoking industry, the traditional cold-smoking kiln is simply a large chimney with ventilators placed up the shaft at intervals, so that draughts can be controlled. The fire is lit in a large hearth either at the foot of the kiln or in a fire pit a few feet away, the smoke being conducted along an underground flue to the kiln by natural draught. At intervals, the positions of the various racks of fish undergoing treatment have to be changed around, so that all the fish receive even smoke treatment. The task of going up a smoke-filled flue is an unpleasant one, so small wonder that the fish-smoking industry is turning to mechanical kilns, where the smoke can be shut off while the fish trolleys are rearranged.

It is a fairly simple matter for the home smoker to construct a kiln on the traditional principle that is simpler in design and sufficient for his needs. For home use, a kiln 180–210 cm (6–7

WOODEN COLD-SMOKER

A Support rods
B Smoke spreader
C Metal plate for fuel
D Brick supports
E Gas ring

MASONRY COLD-SMOKER WITH REMOTE
FIREPIT AND DRAINPIPE SMOKE TUNNEL

WOODEN COLD SMOKER WITH REMOTE FIREPIT AND NATURAL TRENCH SMOKE TUNNEL, COVERED WITH TIN SHEETING AND TURVES feet) high and 60–90 cm (2–3 feet) in width and depth, with a wide open hearth at the bottom, will be adequate, or the principle of the remote fire pit and underground flue can be employed. The kiln may be constructed of stone, brick or, more economically still, concrete blocks, or even wood providing the fire pit is not too close. Tin sheeting should be avoided, as metal is too quickly affected by temperature, and a metal cold-smoker will soon become a hot-smoker when a strong sun shines upon it. The kiln should have a close-fitting door with vent holes 2.5–5 cm (1–2 inches) below the roof, and preferably a perforated plate below the actual smoking chamber to assist an even smoke spread. It should if at all possible stand in a sheltered spot to avoid excessive draughts. An old, disused (of course!) stone or brick outside toilet can be converted into an excellent smoke house and this likeness is often commented on. A Welsh friend, speaking of a smoking kiln at a local estate owner's residence, described it as 'like a *ty bach*' (small house), and a newspaper reporter, in a review of Pinney's famous smokehouse in Suffolk, described the kilns as being 'small, like two smoke-blackened privies'.

The interior must be fitted with some means of suspending the articles to be smoked, either rods supplied with hooks or fittings to accommodate sliding trays.

A thermometer, with one or two spares in case of breakages, will be required, and it is a good idea to buy the kind that will register up to 115°C (240°F), so that it may also be used for hot-smoking. A mechanical kiln thermometer is very expensive. Most household thermometers will only register up to about 49°C (120°F) but a jam thermometer is ideal. Alternatively you could obtain one from a firm that sells laboratory supplies.

OIL CABINET SMOKER

A Gridweld racks   D Supporting bricks
B Dripping tin   E Gas ring
C Metal plate for fuel

So that my own kiln would not be too affected by fluctuating temperatures, I built it inside an old disused dairy with 37 cm (15 inch) thick stone walls, which keeps cool in summer. I would make an infinitely better ballerina than bricklayer, so the building of the kiln was a monumental task. I used concrete blocks and some old bricks I had lying around, made a wooden door frame for the smoking chamber, and tailored an old stable

MASONRY COLD-SMOKER

A Built-in support rods
B Smoke spreader
C Plate for holding fuel

half-door almost to fit the frame. I built against the dairy wall, thereby saving the effort of building a fourth side, and such were the irregularities along the top of its three walls, owing to my inexpertise, that the simple addition of a sheet of loose hardboard provided a roof with adequate ventilation. Nevertheless, it is entirely functional and, unlike a mechanical kiln, is so foolproof and reliable that even I cannot cause it to go wrong.

THE AUTHOR'S COLD-SMOKER, CONCRETE BLOCK
AND BRICK CONSTRUCTION

A Loose hardboard cover
B Built-in support rods (1 cm/⅜ inch steel)
C Hinged wooden door
D Dustbin smoke producer

The building of it is one of my proudest achievements and when a Swedish friend visited me from the gundog world, a sphere in which I have earned a little more acclaim than my building exploits are ever likely to produce, I was able to inform him proudly, 'This is the *Rökhus*.'

My kiln has a large, open hearth, but to place a pile of sawdust in it is somewhat wasteful, as more seems to be consumed than is necessary for smoke production. I burn my sawdust in a galvanized dustbin that can be slid in and out of the hearth. There is a 15 cm (6 inch) hole cut in the side near the bottom of the bin to allow the draught to enter, and to start my fire I tilt the bin and ignite one of my Calor gas rings under the metal of the dustbin floor, which I perforated with a cold chisel.

The two biscuit-tinfuls of sawdust in the bin burn for many hours, and the system of replenishment is similar to that of the chain smoker who lights a new cigarette from the butt of the last. I rake the ash out of the hole with a small shovel, then move the remaining sawdust, which is smouldering at the back of the bin, forward to the hole. I put another tinful of fresh sawdust in behind the old stuff, which quickly ignites the new, then I can go to bed if I so desire, secure in the knowledge that, while I am sleeping, my kiln is working.

HOT-SMOKING KILNS

Pressure smoking

The first piece of smoking equipment I had any experience with was the Abu Smokebox, which is manufactured by Abu Svangsta of Sweden, a famous firm of fishing tackle manufacturers. The Abu measures about 30 x 17.5 x 10 cm (12 x 7 x 4 inches) deep and, on account of its small size, the

DUSTBIN INCINERATOR WHICH CAN BE
PURCHASED FROM HARDWARE STORES. A USEFUL
READY-MADE SMOKE PRODUCING UNIT

potential is very limited. It works on a different principle from
other smoke units, and is said to 'pressure smoke'. A bed of fine
sawdust is spread on its floor and a combined drip tin and wire
rack placed over the sawdust, on which is placed the food to be
smoked. A small methylated spirit burner under the Abu
supplies instant heat, and the sliding lid fits fairly tightly into
place. Here the process differs from other smoking techniques,
which allow for the free passage of smoke out of the top of the
sides of the unit. The smoke has to force its way out of the sides
of the lid, causing smoke pressure inside. High temperatures are
generated within the Abu and the food cooks in the time it takes
for the meths to burn out, which is usually about 20 minutes.

I have no idea just how much heat is generated during the process, but the food smokes and cooks at a far higher temperature than occurs in any other form of hot-smoking. Those who deal in mechanical smoking equipment tend to be somewhat contemptuous of the Abu, stating that it is impossible to achieve adequate smoke penetration with it. While I do have certain reservations about the Abu, I consider that it produces tolerable smoked trout and sausages and is quick and foolproof in operation; but there is one job for which the Abu is unrivalled, which I will go into when discussing smoking quail (see pages 103–106).

I have described Abu smoking for, although its possibilities are limited, you can have a great deal of fun with this device and it does illustrate the basic principle of all hot-smoking units, having a container for the sawdust, a drip tin to catch the drips and so keep the sawdust clean, a rack to support the food, and a source of heat to ignite the sawdust and heat the chamber sufficiently to cook the product.

ORDINARY HOT-SMOKING KILNS

The outside temperature is not a problem for hot-smoking kilns as, should the weather happen to be hot, the kiln will simply require less fuel to maintain its correct temperature, which, in my own case, simply means turning the gas down. For trout, mackerel, eels and sometimes quail, pheasant and domestic ducks, I use hot-smokers constructed from new, unused galvanized dustbins. The bins are bored at intervals so that 9 mm (⅜ inch) steel rods may be inserted. The first pair of rods supports a dripping tin, while higher up three more pairs of rods support moveable wire netting trays. Alternatively, articles

DUSTBIN HOT-SMOKERS

A Wire racks
B Dripping tin
C Loose concrete block hearths
D Bricks which support metal plate which holds fuel
E Gas ring for starting fires and providing additional heat

THE ABU PRESSURE SMOKE BOX

A Sliding lid
B Combined drip tin and wire rack
C Sawdust
D Meths burner

can simply be suspended from rods placed across the top of the
bins, which are then covered to retain the heat and smoke.
Before use, the bins must have smoke passed through them for
at least 12 hours, so that tar deposits can settle on the metal,
which will prevent the first batch of food from becoming metal-
tainted. The bins stand on a hearth constructed of two concrete

blocks, standing on their edges. Four bricks inside the blocks support a piece of sheet metal, in my case corrugated iron beaten flat and perforated. It is on this tin sheet that the sawdust is placed. The fire is started by placing the gas ring under the metal plate. The sawdust, which is placed in a neat pile, about half a biscuit-tinful, soon ignites, and then the gas ring is transferred to the top of the plate, directly under the bottom rim of the bin, this bottom having been well perforated with a cold chisel. It is not necessary for the gas ring to be placed dead centre under the bin to ensure an even heat distribution, and in any case the centre of the plate is covered with sawdust, so it is quite in order for the head of the gas ring to rest just under the bin's edge.

Smoke rises upwards through the perforations in the bottom of the bin, and the gas ring heats the interior, but the dripping tin protects the food from the direct heat of the gas flames. A thermometer, protected by a metal case, is introduced into the kiln via a hole bored in the metal near the top of the kiln. When the required temperature is reached, and the food is placed in the kiln, the temperature will drop, then mount again as the food heats through. You must watch the temperature carefully after about an hour, as by this time the sawdust will be smouldering well and will contribute a certain measure of heat, so the gas must be turned down. This is particularly important in the case of fish, which must never cook too rapidly or at too high a temperature. With flesh or fowl this is by no means so important. If racks are used, the food on the top rack will be ready before the stuff on the lower levels. The top rack must be removed and the lower ones brought up a rung. On account of this, I much prefer to suspend the food than place it on frames, since when suspended it all cooks evenly. A dustbin smoker can accommodate four Aylesbury ducks or 1½ dozen trout or 4 dozen quail if racks are used. Trout can be smoked on racks but, being soft and impressionable, they take the imprint of the wire mesh, which does not detract from their palatability but mars their appearance.

As I do a certain amount of commercial smoking from time to time, I sometimes want to smoke a larger quantity of food than my two dustbin smokers can accommodate. As I was handling a fairly large quantity of ducks, quail and pheasants at one period, I formulated an idea for a cabinet smoker. I submitted plans to two companies and was given some rather high estimates – due to the price of steel, I was told. Not requiring gold-plated smoking kilns, and as I could have bought a 25.2 kg (56 lb) capacity mechanical kiln for not much more than the price they were quoting me, which would have dealt with both cold- and hot-smoked products, I decided the estimates were a little steep, so I acquired a disused oil cabinet for a few pounds. A blacksmith burned or bored holes where I required them, to allow the exit of smoke, to take supporting rods for racks and dripping tins and to enable me to introduce my ubiquitous gas ring to the interior of the cabinet. The structure was covered, inside and out, with a cellular paint, which I burned out by pouring a quantity of methylated spirits into a tray and igniting. Two-thirds of the way up the cabinet was a most convenient shelf, which took four bricks on which I was able to stand a thin steel plate where I could pile my sawdust. A few inches above, there was room for dripping tins, then, higher still, shelves constructed of gridweld on which I could place the articles to be hot-smoked. The gas ring stayed put beneath the steel plate and its sawdust, and ignited the sawdust and heated the smoking chamber. This is a most efficient piece of equipment and can quickly be heated to quite high temperatures if required. It is particularly economical to use and will function on a very low flame, doubtless assisted by the close proximity of the smouldering sawdust to the product. It will take eight ducks or 16 pheasants comfortably.

There are doubtless many other things from which a hot-smoker could be constructed. Wooden barrels are traditional for the production of Arbroath smokies, and I dare say an old electric oven into which some ingenious person has introduced a stream of wood smoke could be a useful tool indeed. If it is hot enough and smoky enough, you have got yourself a hot-smoker.

THE MECHANICAL SMOKER

While on the subject of smoking equipment, perhaps a further word will not be out of place regarding the mechanical smoker referred to earlier, should any home smoker feel inclined to invest in one of these rather elaborate pieces of equipment.

I imagine that all large commercial fish or bacon smoking concerns in Britain will by now have ceased to use traditional equipment and will employ mechanical equipment exclusively. The modern smoker I am acquainted with is the Torry Kiln, which is marketed by Afos Ltd (see page 142). Some of these commercial kilns are very large, costing several thousands of pounds, but the only model with which home smokers might need to concern themselves is the Torry Mini Kiln. This kiln is based on the same principles as the large commercial smoking units, and has a maximum capacity of 25.2 kg (56 lb).

The main advantage the mechanical kiln has over the traditional models is that precise control of temperature, humidity and smoke density can be obtained. Instead of the smoke rising haphazardly upwards, propelled by natural air currents, it is produced in special hearths situated outside the kiln, is circulated horizontally by means of fans or blowers, and is allowed to pass over the products, which are either laid out flat on wire racks stacked one above the other on trolleys or are suspended on rods. The Mini Kiln has four hearths, and the number of fires in use at any one time depends on the type of cure required. Smoke enters the kiln from the hearths via ducts and is first mixed with air. Temperature is maintained by thermostatically controlled electric heaters, and the humidity of the air can be controlled by altering the amount of air intake. The warm air and smoke are then blown by a fan at an even speed over the products arranged on the trolleys in the smoking tunnel. Baffles ensure that the smoke and air are blown evenly across the tunnel. After passing over the product, a proportion of the smoke is led up the chimney but most of it is re-circulated and mixed with fresh smoke and air. Halfway through the smoking process the trolleys are wheeled out and rearranged, as the material nearest to the incoming smoke stream dries out more quickly than the rest.

As the whole smoking process is subjected to rigid control, the Torry Kiln gives a more uniform product than can be obtained by traditional methods. It takes far less time to complete the cure and is not usually so dependent upon prevailing weather conditions.

The Torry Kiln is fitted with instruments to control and measure air speed, humidity and temperature, and a smoke density integrator which controls smoke density, one of the variables of mechanical smoking, according to the product undergoing processing.

The disadvantage of the Torry Kiln, when compared with the traditional kiln, is that it requires more care to maintain it in good working order. Like any other machine, it needs regular cleaning and servicing, and tar and dust may be removed at fairly regular intervals.

OTHER IMPROVISED SMOKERS

Various other improvised smokers can be made. A 40–50 gallon oil drum is particularly well adapted to this purpose. First of all, one end should be cut from the barrel with either a cold chisel or an oxyacetylene torch. The cut-out section should be reduced in size by further trimming so that it finishes up about 7.5 cm (3 inches) less in diameter. This circular plate should have about 20 holes drilled or punched through it, so that it can later be used as a smoke disperser or baffle. The holes allow some of the heat and smoke through, and the rest of the smoke finds its way around the edge of the smoke spreader.

However, before any further conversion is embarked upon, the oil drum must be burned out, so that no taint of oil remains inside. This is best done by pouring a generous quantity of methylated spirits into a wide, flat vessel such as a roasting tin and placing a large piece of rag in the meths to act as a wick. The oil drum should be placed over the meths and tilted slightly so there is a 10 cm (4 inch) gap between the ground and the bottom rim of the drum. The meths should be ignited through this gap and allowed to burn out. A similar technique should be employed for the removal of paint from any other metal article

OIL DRUM SMOKER

A Loose hardboard cover
B Wire mesh racks
C Perforated baffle

D Rack and baffle support
  bars (1cm/⅜inch steel)
E Fire door

that you intend to convert into a smoker, as paint would also taint the product.

To support the smoke spreader, four holes should be drilled in the wall of the drum about 45 cm (18 inches) from the closed end. You can either put long bolts through these holes, securing them by nuts so that about 10 cm (4 inches) of the bolts protrude into the chamber, allowing the smoke spreader to rest upon them, or you can simply position the holes so that two long metal rods can be used as supports instead of the fixed bolts. A series of corresponding holes should be drilled in the

REFRIGERATOR CONVERSION COLD-SMOKER

A Roof vent
B Racks
C Smoke spreader
D Metal plate for fuel
E Brick supports

wall of the drum so other metal rods can be inserted, their function being to support the smoking racks. Here there are no hard and fast rules. It is up to the individual to decide how many racks there will be and how far apart they will lie, according to the type of food you wish to smoke. I think it is a good idea to make provision for four racks about 12.5 cm (5 inches) apart. You are then in a position to leave one or more racks out when smoking bulkier objects.

The cutting torch or chisel should then be used to cut a fire hole near the base of the drum. This should measure 30 x 30 cm (12 x 12 inches) for easy fuelling and the removal of ash. It should reach right to the base of the drum and leave no edge or lip to hinder cleaning-out operations. It is quite feasible to operate this type of smoker with a permanently open fire hole, but if a hinged door is fitted to the hole this will give you far greater control of draught, heat and smoke.

The racks that will rest on the loose metal rods inside the drum and support the food being processed should be circular to give maximum area and should measure about 2.5 cm (1 inch) less in diameter than the barrel. The outside rim should be of strong steel and the bottom should be of strong welded mesh about 2.5 cm (1 inch) square for general purposes, or fine wire screens for smoking of such things as shellfish, nuts or bilberries. A pair of strong handles on either side of the racks will greatly facilitate handling.

To cover the top of the drum, use either a sheet of heavy plywood, a sheet of metal or a piece of asbestos, either flat or corrugated. It is a simple enough matter to insert a stick under this cover in various positions to control smoke and heat escape.

To start the fire, you can stack sawdust around a perforated

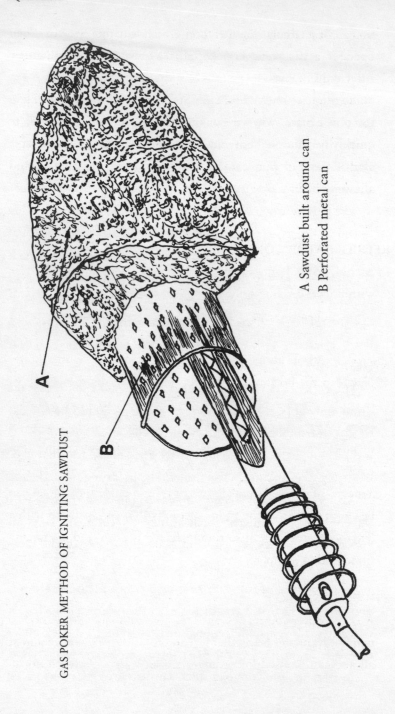

GAS POKER METHOD OF IGNITING SAWDUST

A Sawdust built around can
B Perforated metal can

tin can or a circular kitchen food grater, leaving the nearest end open. If a gas poker is inserted, the sawdust quickly ignites. Alternatively, an ordinary gas ring can be covered with a 20 cm (8 inch) square metal sheet and the sawdust piled around and on top of the plate. When the gas ring is ignited, the covering plate quickly becomes red hot and starts the fire. Once the sawdust is alight, the gas ring can be removed from the sawdust and allowed to burn independently as an additional source of heat should the drum smoker be required for hot-smoking.

REFRIGERATOR CONVERSION

An old, disused upright-type refrigerator makes a useful smoker within certain limitations. It is well insulated and so will conserve heat but, by the nature of its original function, is not designed to withstand heat, so it is only suitable as a cold-smoker. A hole about 25 cm (10 inches) square or round should be cut in the bottom of the fridge, which should be raised off the ground and supported on a square built of concrete blocks, open at the front to allow the fire to be placed within the square of blocks. Alternatively, the device can be used in conjunction with the remote fire pit and underground smoke tunnel and, as a means of draught control, two or three 5 cm (2 inch) holes can be cut in the top of the fridge. Better still, it can be fitted with a length of stovepipe, protruding from the top and preferably fitted with a damper.

THE SHED SMOKER

A shed conversion makes a very useful cold-smoker, one of its major advantages being that it requires hardly any conversion at all and can be used for ordinary storage purposes when not in

FISH FILLETS STRUNG AND HUNG ON HAZEL STICKS
SUPPORTED BY 15 CM/6 INCH NAILS IN SHED SMOKER RAFTERS

use as a smoker. Another advantage is that, as a shed is
normally built with adequate headroom, there is plenty of space
to work in. Racks can easily be suspended from the roof or,
alternatively, 15 cm (6 inch) nails can be driven into the rafters
to support 1.2 cm (½ inch) hazel rods. Sides of salmon can be
suspended from the rods by strings threaded under the lug
bones (the hard triangular plates to which the pectoral fins are
attached) and under the shoulder plates, which are situated a
few inches above the lug bones (according to the size of the fish,
of course), directly behind the gill covers.

You will need to build a hearth in the middle of the floor of
the shed smoker, which can best be done by using three sides of
a square of loose bricks or concrete blocks as a base, on which

a square sheet of metal should be rested. A three-sided wall of loose bricks or blocks can be constructed around the sides of the metal plate to contain the sawdust or chips. A perforated metal or plywood sheet can be placed above the fuel to act as a smoke disperser. It is a simple matter to light the fire by lighting a gas ring underneath the metal plate of the hearth, which soon becomes red hot and ignites the fuel.

Various other devices can also be used, including a metal dustbin incinerator. These can actually be purchased ready perforated, for burning garden rubbish. The unperforated kind can simply have a 12.5 cm (5 inch) hole cut at ground level for draught, with a perforated lid, and is ignited by tilting it on one side, the lighted gas ring being placed under the bottom rim near the draught hole. The only other alteration the shed smoker requires to make it fully operative is a small space (about 5 cm/2 inches is sufficient) under the door, made by cutting a small amount of wood away, to allow the intake of air. This can easily be covered by nailing a 10 cm (4 inch) board over the gap when the smoker is not being used as such. Most sheds have a space of about 2.5 cm (1 inch) between the walls and the eaves, which will allow for the escape of smoke, but failing this a few holes can be bored under the eaves.

Another advantage of the shed smoker is that it makes an excellent drying room in which to hang salmon or any other food, after brining and prior to smoking. A disadvantage is that, if smoke should be seen escaping from a wooden shed by a casual observer who is unaware of the operation in hand, the matter might well be misconstrued and the local fire brigade could possibly be called out on a fruitless errand.

8 Cold-smoked products

SMOKED SALMON

There are three varieties of wild salmon with which we who live
in the Western hemisphere should concern ourselves. Reputedly
king of them all is the Atlantic salmon, the fish that runs up the
rivers to spawn in Norway, Finland, Great Britain and Ireland
and the rivers on the eastern seaboard of the United States and
Canada. This is the fish that is famous the world over as a
sporting and culinary proposition and is commonly associated
with social prestige and affluence. There is no question that the
Atlantic salmon is a very fine fish but perhaps its illustrious
connections give it a somewhat unfair advantage over its Pacific
cousins.

The main groups of Pacific salmon consist of the sockeye, the
pink, the cohoe and the keta, also known as the chum or
silverbright. Of these four we can virtually discount the sockeye
in Britain, as catches of this fish are absorbed by the canning
industry. The pink, which can be readily identified by the hump
on its back, is seldom seen in this country either, except in a tin,
so we are left with the cohoe and the keta.

The cohoe is a stocky fish, deep in proportion to its length
and lacking the streamlined, torpedo-like form of our own
Atlantic salmon. The flesh of the cohoe is a rather deep

orangey-pink in colour, deeper hued than the pink flesh of the Atlantic salmon and somewhat scorned in some quarters on account of its 'inferior' colour. The cohoe is, nevertheless, a very good fish, although very tender to handle when frozen and thawed out again. It has a very slightly sweetish taste when smoked, which is not at all unpleasant.

The keta salmon is a very similar fish to the cohoe in outward colour and shape but is somewhat paler fleshed. They are occasionally confused by the commercial packers, as I have sometimes found a cohoe thrown in with a batch of ketas when purchasing salmon for smoking. When this occurs I accept it as a bonus, as the cohoe is higher priced than the keta. The keta has a flesh colour similar to that of the Atlantic salmon, although, all things being equal, it has a lower fat content than the Atlantic and cohoe varieties. Cooked in the traditional manner, it is rather tasteless compared with the other two but can, with care, make an excellent smoked product. In fact, without any attempt at deception on my part, I have frequently had my smoked keta mistaken for Scotch salmon.

If I were to make a choice, I would prefer a fresh-run Atlantic salmon to any other, but not every Atlantic salmon caught is by any means a fresh-run fish. Many rod-caught fish have lain a long time in low water or have battled their way past innumerable obstacles, have lost condition, and are what the smoker terms 'dry fish'. This situation never arises with imported Pacific salmon. All fish are caught by commercial fisheries at the mouths of the rivers, so every Pacific salmon is a fresh-run fish and superior in quality to a tired Scottish fish taken late in the summer.

I picked up a very useful tip from an experienced hotelier

regarding the treatment of frozen Pacific salmon. As some of the oil is lost during freezing, oil must be fed back into the fish to achieve the best results. I do this by painting the fillets with olive oil half way through the 24-hour air-drying period, which falls between brining and placing in the kiln.

Farmed salmon varies greatly in quality and you will probably have to shop around until you find a product you like. It can be excellent to eat, but muscle tone is flaccid compared to wild fish, which continually exercise their bodies in the normal course of their existence. Farmed salmon may tear under its own weight when hung, so it is recommended that the fillets are smoked flat on wire racks.

Filleting

A very sharp, thin-bladed knife with a pliable blade is required for this operation. I use one made by J. Marttiini, of Finland, which is available at most gun and fishing tackle shops.

In the case of whole salmon, the fish must first be gutted, slitting the underside from the vent to the lug bones. The blood channel must then be removed from the back of the gut cavity. The membrane should be broken by the forefinger and the

FINNISH FILLETING KNIFE

ENGLISH FISH FILLETING KNIFE

METHOD OF FILLETING A FISH

blood channel taken out, preferably under a running tap. There are several large veins present in the belly walls of the fish and these will turn black during smoking unless punctured and squeezed out. If these veins are ignored, they will not affect the flavour or keeping qualities of the fish but detract somewhat from the appearance.

To fillet the fish, leave the head on as it provides something

A Incision under shoulder plate
B Incision under lug bone

A

B

SIDE OF SALMON (FLESH SIDE)

SIDE OF SALMON (SKIN SIDE)

A SPLIT FISH (ALTERNATIVE METHOD TO FILLETING)

to get hold of. The neck should be cut through until the spine is reached, as close to the head as possible, leaving the hard shoulder plates intact as these are necessary to assist in the hanging of the fillets or sides. The knife blade should be turned at right angles, so the flat of the blade lies parallel to the length of the spine. You will find it easier if the back of the fish is towards you. A straight cut should be made, slicing through the ribs where they join the spine, cutting the entire length of the fish with the knife blade held all the way at right angles to the length of the body. The large dorsal fin can cause trouble, so the blade must be fractionally raised to pass above this obstacle when it is reached and the same applies to the anal fin lower down. When the first side is freed, the fish should be turned over. This may be harder to remove than the first, as the remaining side has acted as a supporting cushion when removing the first side.

The ribs can either be left intact until the sides are smoked or can be removed at this stage by taking them out along with a thin layer of flesh. I favour the former course in the case of frozen salmon, as I believe the less the sides are disturbed before smoking the better, to avoid damage.

A slit should be cut behind the shoulder plates and lug bones, through which to thread string to hang the sides by. Some authorities suggest that the skin of the fish should be scored in three places, directly over the thickest parts of the fish to assist salt penetration; but in my experience this is entirely unnecessary, and undesirable as it disfigures the side.

An alternative method to filleting, which is sometimes preferred in the case of small fish, is splitting. The whole, ungutted fish is split down the back, including the head, and the guts and blood channel are removed, leaving the belly intact. The spine is taken out, save for 7.5 cm (3 inches) of the tail, which is left to strengthen the fish during subsequent handling, as the fish is smoked suspended by the tail. After pre-salting, a suitable stick is passed through cuts behind the lug bones, to keep the fish opened up. The eyes and gills are also removed.

Pre-salting or brining

If dry-salting is favoured, the fish is well washed in cold water, then rubbed with fine salt. The sides are laid on a bed of salt 2.5 cm (1 inch) thick in a suitable receptacle. A 1.2 cm (½ inch) layer of salt is spread on the body of the side, but with only a sprinkling towards the tail. The other side is laid skin down on the first, and another 1.2 cm (½ inch) layer of salt is spread on top. The time required in the salt obviously varies according to the size of the fish and the fat content. Here I find myself at variance with any previous information I have read on the subject. It is suggested that sides from salmon varying between 3.58 and 10.7 kg (8 and 24 lb) should be salted from 12 to 36 hours. This is far too long; I consider the resulting product to be inedible and would advocate reducing these salting times by half. After salting, the sides should be well washed to remove surface salt and should feel springy and firm to the touch. The fish should then be hung up to drip for 24 hours, preferably at a room temperature of about 18–21°C (65–70°F).

During dry-salting, the sides will lose 8–9% in weight, and wastage through gutting and filleting will probably amount to about 25%.

Brining

This is my favoured method. An 80% brine is prepared (1.2 kg/2 lb 10¾ oz of salt to 4.54 litres/1 gallon of water) and the sides are totally immersed for periods varying from 1 hour to 3 hours, according to size and fat content. Frozen salmon require less than fresh fish on account of oil loss. I once prepared a 3 kg (7 lb) September hen fish in poor condition, very red and distended with spawn. I was asked by the clients to salt it lightly, as commercial salt cures always seemed to be too salty for their tastes. I brined this fish for only 50 minutes and this was entirely to their palates.

The brined fish should be hung up, unwashed. In my opinion it is even more preferable to hang the fish up to dry for 24 hours than in the case of dry-salted fish, as the sides will only lose 1½–3% weight during brining. Brined fish, hung in the manner described, will form a good salt gloss, which adds to their appearance.

Smoking

Prior to dry-salting or brining, at least one side should be weighed and the weight recorded. The finished product must lose 17–18% in weight, so you must do a sum and work out what weight 17–18% is of the whole, subtract this from the whole, and the answer is what the smoked side should weigh. So under traditional methods, which depend to a certain extent on atmospheric humidity and ambient temperatures, smoking time required is not therefore a matter of so many hours but until the product has dropped to the correct weight. This is likely to take from 24 to 60 hours and I have even heard of salmon smoking for 4 days. Smoke temperatures should be about 26°C (80°F), never higher than 32°C (90°F).

Storage

When the salmon has finished smoking, it should not be eaten immediately but should be allowed to mature for at least 24 hours. According to the Norwegians, a salmon should be caught on a Thursday, smoked over the weekend and eaten the following Wednesday.

Smoked salmon has a fairly good shelf life under conditions of ordinary refrigeration – about a week, with a 10-day maximum. However, it is a commodity that freezes particularly well, so there is no need to push it to its limit of keeping time. It can be either cut into pieces, on the skin, or cut into slices, wrapped in aluminium foil and frozen.

COLD-SMOKED TROUT

Many anglers fish lakes and reservoirs for large trout, usually rainbows. These fish are sometimes less than prime specimens. I am no expert on marine biology but under some conditions it would appear that the fish wish to spawn but are unable to do so. They produce normal quantities of spawn and milt, which, as it is not used, is absorbed into the system again. The fish turn an unpleasant colour and the actual flesh tends to turn pale, so the best possible destination for this type is the inside of a cold-smoking kiln. Needless to say, prime fish, as always, will produce a superior finished product, particularly in appearance, but this is still the best method to utilize poorer-quality trout.

The fish should be gutted and beheaded and the blood channel along the inside of the spine removed. It should be split, as illustrated on page 67, by placing the fish on its back and cutting through one set of ribs as close to the spine as possible, slicing right down through the flesh almost to the skin of the back. The trout should be brined in 80% solution for a rather elastic period depending on size, usually 2–4 hours for a 900 g–1.8 kg (2–4 lb) fish or more for larger specimens. Care must be taken over hanging, as trout flesh is very tender, but the best method, after washing in cold water, is to drive a meat hook right through the top of the spine about 2.5 cm (1 inch) below the end. A second hook should then be passed under the lug bone on the opposite side. The hook through the spine will support the entire weight of the fish and the other one will keep the fish opened when it is hung on a rail.

The fish should be allowed to drip, preferably overnight, then smoked in exactly the same way as salmon at 21–26°C (70–80°F). Weight loss should be slightly more than salmon sides, around 20%. Smoking time varies according to size and atmospheric humidity but I find they are usually ready in 24–36 hours.

Unlike salmon, the smoked surface of the fish does not form a rind. It is soft and glazed, like smoked haddock or cod, and can be sliced off and eaten along with the rest, after the spine and ribs have been removed with a sharp filleting knife. Cold-smoked trout is an excellent substitute for smoked salmon and should be served in exactly the same way. Some of my patrons even consider it to be superior.

Storage

See smoked salmon.

SMOKED FILLETS OF BEEF

Some time ago, I had a commercial association with a North Country farmer who, as an expanding sideline, had a smoked food business, supplying many first-class hotels, mainly in the western half of the country. He did not process smoked foods himself but had it custom smoked for him by people like myself. He was particularly keen to put smoked beef on the market – what type or how processed, he did not specify. The idea was left in abeyance for some time, as in any case I was fairly well occupied in smoking ducks, quail and pheasants for him, and it was not until the matter of smoked beef was raised by a first-class butcher of my acquaintance, who had enjoyed my smoked quail, that I pursued it further.

As I have already mentioned, the smoking of new products, about which there is no available literature, depends to a great extent on experimentation and intelligent guesswork. It is

FILLET OF BEEF, HUNG

seldom one gets a new product 100% correct the first time, and beef is an expensive commodity to use as a subject for experiments. I mentioned this point to my butcher friend, who airily waved my caution aside, offering me a box of frozen fillets of beef on which to experiment. For a first attempt, they turned out very well, although at the outset I was not sure whether I should make a cold-smoked or a hot-smoked product out of them. I did discover that a period in cold smoke was quite sufficient to smoke the fillets right through, and the result was such that I can recommend without hesitation that they should be treated as a cold-smoked meat and always eaten raw, like smoked salmon.

Smoking

The fillets do not need to be of first-class quality. Cow fillets are quite adequate, as are those from cattle that have not been 'done' well in the store period and have finally been finished off on grass, possibly going to market as beef cattle a good deal older than would normally be the case. Such beef is covered with a good layer of fat but the lean is dark and sinewy, without the 'marbling' of fat between the tissues. Only the thick bottom part of the fillet should be used. The tail end of the fillet tends to go dry during smoking – it is best used for steak Châteaubriand and should be served sliced along the grain, in the Dutch manner, instead of across.

The fillets should be pricked right through with a fork in several places on either side, to allow the brine to penetrate. Most of the fat should be removed as this hinders both brine and smoke penetration and, unless the beef has been dead for at least a week, the brine cannot penetrate the flesh and the resulting product will taste comparatively insipid.

The fillets should be covered in 80% brine and allowed to soak for 2½–3½ hours, according to thickness and fat content. After brining, a thin piece of string should be tied tightly around the smaller end of the fillet, about 5 cm (2 inches) from the end, and a loop formed for hanging in the kiln (see illustration).

The beef should be hung to drip and cure for 24 hours before it is placed in the smoke house. As with all cold-smoked products, a beef fillet must lose a certain amount of moisture, and consequently weight, before it can be considered properly smoke-cured. The fillets should therefore be weighed before brining and a calculation made as to what the approximate smoked weight should finally be, working on my principle of a required weight loss of 20–25%. During smoking, temperatures must never exceed 26°C (80°F) or the beef will case harden too rapidly, preventing the escape of moisture. Low smoke temperatures do not appear to make any difference to the final product, but if the beef is smoked at a temperature of 10–15°C (50–60°F), it will obviously take longer, as of course it will in times of high relative humidity. Nevertheless I find that 5–8 days in the kiln is normally sufficient. It is as well to bear in mind that the fuller the kiln, the longer any product will take, as more moisture has to be evaporated, so it is a good idea never to fill kilns to maximum capacity and to leave a good air space around every article.

The beef will begin to turn black after about 2½ days of smoking, which is as things should be. Beef is a tolerant material and, should the fire go out in the kiln at any time, the product will not suffer until such time as the fire is re-lit and the flow of smoke begins again. I mention this point as, when a kiln is working for a period of up to a week or beyond, natural human laxity is such that the fire is far more likely to go out than if the kiln should be working for only a couple of days.

Towards the end of the smoking period, the beef should be tested by weighing and, if all seems in order, the final test should be applied. This consists of slicing almost through the fillet at its thickest part, in order to give it the visual test. The freshly cut surfaces should have a dull, matt finish, proving adequate smoke penetration and drying. If the appearance is still bright and shiny yet the weight loss seems about right, another 48 hours in the smoke will conclude the matter. It is also worth remembering that if either beef or salmon should prove to be particularly stubborn over losing weight during an excessively humid period, they can be taken out of the kiln, allowed to 'sweat' for around 12 hours in the case of salmon and around 24 hours for beef, then re-smoked until correct weight loss is achieved.

Storage

Smoked fillet of beef has a long shelf life in a refrigerator. It is still good after 3 weeks and could well be for considerably longer, particularly in the case of a whole uncut fillet, but again I think it is better to wrap it in aluminium foil and freeze, as it loses nothing in the process. Smoked fillet forms a hard, savoury rind on its outside, which can be eaten or trimmed off according to taste, as in the case of the smoked surface of a side of salmon. In common with other smoked products, beef should be allowed to mature for 24 hours before being eaten, then should be thinly sliced across the grain and eaten as a starter as an alternative to smoked salmon. Lemon juice is a suitable additive, and smoked beef between brown bread and butter is one of my favourite sandwiches.

A smoked fillet, or part of one, can be placed in an oven for 1 hour at a temperature of 115°C (240°F/Gas Mark ¼–½), allowed to cool, then eaten. The result cannot be considered as anything but good but the whole character is completely altered and, for my own palate, I much prefer the cold uncooked smoked beef.

KIPPERS

The herring, which of course is what the kipper is before it is processed, is seldom the quarry of the sea angler in Britain. The

Swedes and the Norwegians traditionally fish for herrings with hand lines from small boats at the mouths of their fjords, often making good catches, particularly when night fishing. Nevertheless, although as a British home smoker you are unlikely to catch your own herrings, if you live close to a port where these fish are landed you may well decide to smoke your own kippers. If so, you will be able to make certain that you obtain only the freshest of fish.

Smoking

The herrings should first be washed well to remove loose scales, then split from the head, right down the back, and the gut and roe should be removed. After splitting, the fish should be washed again to remove any bits of gut or blood.

Well-conditioned, medium-sized fish should be brined for 15 minutes in 70% brine. Extra large herrings require 20–30 minutes and if the fish are lean, e. g. 'spent herrings' (fish that have spawned), 10 minutes in the brine will be sufficient.

The best way to hang kippers for their pre-drying period and indeed in the smoke house is by employing 'tenter sticks', which are wooden battens fitted with small hooks. However, these are not essential and here a little human ingenuity can be brought in. They should be hung to drip for 1 hour. Longer drying periods are not required, as 'salt gloss' does not play such a large part in the appearance of the finished product – gloss in kippers depends to a greater extent on the natural oil within the fish, which comes to the surface during smoking.

During smoking, temperatures should be around 26°C (80°F), never more than 29°C (85°F) until possibly the last half hour, when the temperature can be increased to 35°C (95°F) in order to develop a deeper hue and to bring the oil gloss to the surface of the fish.

Smoking time depends upon the usual factors, i. e. size of fish, quantity in kiln, atmospheric humidity, etc. But as a guideline I can suggest between 6 and 18 hours. As with all cold-smoked products, however, weight loss is the surest guide, and from the fresh, split condition the fish should lose 14–18% in weight.

Storage

Keeping time is governed by weight loss and varies from 4 to 7 days, bearing in mind that the higher the weight loss, the longer the shelf life.

SMOKED COD ROES

Cod roes may be processed from either the fresh article or from frozen roes. They are extremely delicate, and musy be handled very carefully as their fine transparent skins rupture very easily – their handling is a major part of the technique. They must first be carefully washed in cold water then immersed in 70% brine for about 1 hour.

SMOKING

A major problem is how to suspend the roes for pre-drying and subsequent smoking. If they are large enough and sufficiently firm, a piece of string can be tied around the bisection of the roe. If you are in any doubt as to whether the roes will stand this treatment they can be laid on racks, but a disadvantage of this method is that they take the imprint of the racks rather heavily and appearance suffers. Whichever method is used, the roes

COD ROE STRUNG FOR SMOKING

should pre-dry for half an hour before being placed in the kiln, where they should be smoked at 26–29°C (80–85°F) for between 12 and 24 hours, according to the usual conditions. The final product is firm, easily sliced and an attractive dark red colour. Weight loss should be approximately 25% of the original weight before brining.

Storage

Smoked cod roes will keep for about a week in the fridge or can be well wrapped and frozen.

FINNAN HADDOCK

Fairly small haddock of about 450 g (1 lb) in weight are ideal for processing into finnan haddock. The fish must be carefully gutted, as small haddock are very tender and tear easily. The heads are removed and the gut cavity is scraped and cleaned. The fish are then split all the way along the inside of the spine, from the neck to the tail fin, care being taken not to cut into the skin of the back. The opened-out fish are then soaked in 80%

brine for 7–15 minutes, depending on size; a 450 g (1 lb) fish will require 10 minutes' brining.

After brining they are hung on tenter sticks for about 6 or 7 hours, as a good salt gloss is important to the finished product. Smoked haddock are particularly subject to case hardening so they should be protected from any strong drying winds during this period.

Smoking

The finnans should be smoked at 26°C (80°F) for a period of 6 to 12 hours, and should be removed before the full colour is reached, as this full colour will develop within a few hours of cooling. Required weight loss is 12–14%.

There is a slight variation of the process described for the production of 'straws'. Here smaller haddock are used, not in excess of 335 g (12 oz) in weight. The preparation is exactly the same as for finnans until brining, which takes only 4–5 minutes in the 80% brine. After drying, the fish are smoked from 4 to 8 hours at 26°C (80°F), and the final product should have a pale straw colour. Weight loss should be 8–12%.

Storage

Finnan haddock should be well wrapped and frozen after smoking.

SMOKED SHRIMPS

Shrimps can be cold-smoked either whole or as peeled meats. For the former method, the shrimps should have their heads removed and be washed and left to drain for 30 minutes. They are then brined for 30–60 minutes (according to preference) in 40% brine (535 g/1 lb 3 oz salt to 4.54 litres/1 gallon of water), then boiled in the brine or in plain water, again according to taste, for 30 minutes. The shrimps are then allowed to air-dry on racks for 2 hours.

Alternatively, clean peeled meats may be boiled for 1–4 minutes, depending on size, in a 40% brine. They are then allowed to drain on oiled wire mesh trays until the surface of the meat is dry.

Smoking

The shrimps are then placed in the kiln and smoking is carried out for 1–1½ hours at a temperature of 26°C (80°F). The yield of smoked meats after shelling is approximately 36% of the whole raw shrimp weight.

Prawns can be prepared and smoked in the same way.

Storage

Shrimps and prawns should be well wrapped and frozen after smoking.

BLOATERS

Bloaters are produced from whole, ungutted, slightly salted herrings, and owe their distinctive flavour to the enzymes or ferments in the gut. The herrings are mixed with solid salt for about 12 hours, after which the surface salt is removed by soaking the fish in fresh water for 20 minutes. They are threaded on rods, either through the mouth and gills or through the eyes. As it is not necessary to produce a salt gloss, the fish do not require a dripping and air-drying period and can be placed in the kiln straight away.

Smoking

The total smoking period in the traditional smoke house is about 12 hours (4 hours in the Torry Kiln). The smoking temperature should be maintained at 25°C (77°F), and for exactly half the smoking period the bloaters should be dried with an absolute minimum of smoke. For the remainder of the smoking period, very dense smoke should be produced, which gives the fish a mild smoky flavour while the product retains a bright silvery appearance.

Storage

The bloaters should lose only about 6% weight, so consequently keeping time is short – about 2–3 days.

RED HERRINGS

Besides herring, the raw material may be pilchard and sprat. They are placed in solid salt in a suitable bucket or vat-shaped receptacle for 7–8 days, the bulk ratio of salt to fish being about 1:2. Surface salt is removed by soaking in fresh water for 1 hour.

Smoking

The fish are cold smoked for 5–6 days at a temperature of 29°C (85°F).

Storage

Weight loss is 20–25% and the fish will keep for several months without refrigeration.

SMOKED BACON

Bacon may be cured by either brining or dry-salting. The traditional method appears to vary from one county to another in Britain. For example, dry-salting is traditional in the Lincolnshire Fen district, whereas Galloway, in south-west Scotland, favours brining.

Salt should be applied at a rate of 450 g (1 lb) per 4.5 kg (10 lb) meat. Half the salt should be rubbed well into the meat 5 days after killing – no sooner or the meat will not absorb the cure. As pork taints very easily, it is most important that the meat should be kept cool during this waiting period. The other half of the dry cure should be applied after 3 days. The bacon should be allowed to cure at a rate of 2 days per 450 g (1 lb) of flesh – e. g. 5.4 kg (12 lb) must cure for 24 days, after which time the bacon must be removed from the salt and any of the cure adhering to the surface should be brushed off and the bacon kept quite dry. Bacon cured in this manner would keep at room temperature for considerable periods, suspended from rafters, in the days before refrigeration came into general use.

Sweet pickle brine (see page 27) should be used for a brine cure, and the meat should remain in the pickle for the same length of time, i. e. 2 days per 450 g (1 lb), and should be agitated and turned every 2 days. After brining, the bacon should be well washed and hung up to drain in a cool place for 48 hours.

Both dry-cured and brine-cured bacon is now ready for smoking, if desired. The length of the smoking period varies according to individual taste. Temperatures should be 24–26°C (75–80°F) and can vary from 24 hours for a very mild smoke flavour to 7 days for a stronger smoke cure.

SMOKED HAM

Ham is thicker than bacon, so penetration by either sweet

pickle or dry cure takes longer: 3 days per 450 g (1 lb) should be allowed. If the brine cure is used, it is a good idea to inject around the bone with the brine pump (see pages 28–29) before the ham is totally immersed in the pickle, after which it should be turned every 2 days and the brine must be stirred. The rule applies about temperature as in all protracted cures, namely that it is far safer to keep it at around 1.5°C (35°F). After the curing period, the ham should be washed and hung up to drain at around 3°C (38°F) for 48 hours.

Like bacon, the time the ham should be smoked varies according to taste. It should be smoked at a temperature of 21–26°C (70–80°F) for a period varying from 48 hours to 6 weeks. In the case of the longer period, smoking does not need to be continuous. The fire may be lit intermittently, and during this period slices of ham may be cut off and eaten, the remainder staying inside the smoke house for further smoking. I understand that a similar system was used in old-fashioned chimneys in Germany, which had small doors in them a few feet from the ground for easy access. Smoked sausages and other meat were simply stored in the chimney until required.

Ham prepared in this manner can also be hot-smoked at 104–121°C (220–250°F), and will require a cooking period of 5–7 hours, according to size.

STORAGE

Bacon and ham can simply be hung up in a kitchen or larder, as long as the room is fairly cool. Alternatively, store them in the fridge. Traditionally they last from one year to the next, but I wouldn't advise pushing it this far.

SMOKED EGGS

This is a little-known method but of all the smoked foods the flavour of smoked eggs is unique. New-laid eggs should be avoided, as they can be extremely difficult to remove from the shell when boiled, so it is better to use eggs that are about a week old.

The eggs should be hard-boiled by placing them in cold water and bringing to the boil. When boiling point is reached, the pan should be removed from the heat and allowed to cool for 15 minutes. The water should be drained off and, after the eggs have cooled down, the shells should be removed. The eggs are well sprinkled with table salt and white pepper, then placed on wire racks in the cold smoker and smoked at about 26°C (80°F) for about 12 hours, by which time they should have turned deep amber. They may be sliced and eaten in sandwiches, served in salads with mayonnaise or used as hors d'oeuvre when dusted with paprika. They are also used in my recipe for smoked rabbit pie (see page 129).

Storage

The eggs should be kept in the fridge and eaten within a few days.

SMOKED NUTS

Most kinds of nuts are suitable for smoking – almonds, either whole or blanched, walnuts, brazils, chestnuts, hazelnuts and pistachio nuts. Place them on fine wire gauze screens. Some people say nuts cannot stand heavy smoking and advocate a smoking time of 2–3 hours at 24–29°C (75–85°F), but this is a matter of taste and I prefer them smoked for 10–12 hours.

Storage

Store the nuts in an airtight tin.

SMOKED CHEESE

Few people can be unfamiliar with Austrian smoked cheese, a commercially available product in a sausage-like form. Recently cheese manufacturers have begun to smoke other types of cheese, including English ones such as Wensleydale. During the processing of Austrian smoked cheese, the milk from which it is manufactured is first smoked, then made into cheese, no further smoking process being involved. As cheese making is probably beyond the scope or inclination of the average home smoker, the cheese must be smoked in the piece.

First of all, any rind or protective wax, plastic or muslin coating must be removed. Any kind of mild cheese can be smoked. Danish Blue, Gorgonzola, Stilton and Camembert are not suitable.

To allow for maximum smoke penetration, the cheese should be cut into pieces not more than 4 cm (1½ inches) thick. Smoking is best carried out at the lower temperature ranges – 15°C (60°F) is ideal. Again, opinions vary on how long the cheese requires smoking. According to some, 2 hours in light smoke is all that is required, but I prefer a period of 5–6 hours.

Storage

After smoking, the cheese should be wrapped in aluminium foil and kept under refrigeration until required. To obtain the finest flavour from smoked cheese it should be left at room temperature for about 3 hours before eating.

SMOKED BILBERRIES OR WHINBERRIES

The berries must be firm in texture and not over-ripe, otherwise the keeping qualities of the finished product will be impaired. The berries should be placed on a fine wire mesh rack and cold-smoked at 24–29°C (75–85°F) until they lose moisture and the skins take on a wrinkled appearance, rather like dried raisins. Smoking time will depend on atmospheric humidity and appearance must be accepted as a guide.

Smoked bilberries are excellent accompanied by ice cream or clotted cream.

Storage

The smoked berries should be stored in a refrigerator in a covered but not airtight vessel. Use within a few days.

SMOKED SAUSAGES

It would be possible to write a whole book on sausages and still fail to cover the subject in its entirety. So many different types of sausage are made in so many different parts of the world. Recipes vary from county to county, from province to province, and from country to country and continent to continent. As this is the case, I do not propose to go too deeply into sausage making but will describe one type only. For the large manufacture of sausages, special equipment is essential in the form of mincing machines, mixing vats and filling machines. Simpler sausage machines are now available for domestic use, and the casings can be obtained by mail order (see page 143). However, home smokers who plan to undertake only a once-a-year sausage-making excursion would be well advised to make do with a minimum of equipment and to enlist professional help in the form of a friendly butcher over certain phases of the process.

This is the recipe for an excellent smoked sausage.

> 2.7 kg (6 lb) lean beef and 1.8 kg (4 lb) pork (preferably 50/50 fat and lean)
>
> or 2.25 kg (5 lb) venison or elk and 2.25 kg (5 lb) pork (50/50 fat and lean)
>
> 40 g (1½ oz) white pepper
>
> 55 g (2 oz) salt
>
> ½ tablespoon garlic powder (if available)
>
> 7 g (¼ oz) whole black peppercorns
>
> 570 ml (1 pint) red wine

The beef or venison is cut into pieces approximately 6 cm (2½ inches) square and placed in a vessel containing sweet pickle brine (see page 27). Keep refrigerated at 1.5°C (35°F) for about 10 days, and agitate and stir well every third day. The meat is then removed, washed, and placed on wire mesh racks to dry, still under refrigeration, for 24 hours.

When the beef has dried thoroughly, the pork is cut into pieces small enough to go into the mincer. Both pork and beef pieces are placed in a large mixing bowl. The pepper, salt and garlic powder are added and the ingredients thoroughly mixed.

The meat is now put through the mincer twice, using cutters that will produce a medium to coarse texture. The peppercorns and red wine are now added to the minced meat and the contents of the bowl are thoroughly mixed and allowed to stand for 2 days. The butcher should then be asked to stuff the sausages, using casings that will allow for a sausage about 45 cm

(18 inches) in length and 5 cm (2 inches) in diameter. The stuffed sausages are left hanging in a refrigerator for 2 days.

The sausages are now ready for smoking. They should be hung in the smokehouse vertically and smoked at a temperature of 29–35°C (85–95°F) for 14–16 hours.

After the smoking process follows the maturing process, during which the sausages are kept at 1.5°C (35°F) for 2 weeks. At the end of this period, they will have lost about 50% of their original weight.

Storage

The sausages should be kept in a cool, dry larder or under refrigeration, and are ready to eat without further cooking. Eat within a week or so.

9   Hot-smoked products

SMOKED TROUT

There are three varieties of trout that might concern the smoker. Commonest of all is the rainbow, which is delicious when hot-smoked. This fish is the mainstay of the commercial trout farm, reproducing easily and growing well under reasonable conditions. It is an ideal fish for stocking lakes and reservoirs but will not normally stay put in rivers. It can be an excellent sporting and eating fish, with a delicate flavour, but quality varies considerably, and you will have to shop around until you find the farm that supplies the best fish.

Some trout farms have the American brook trout. This fish is wider across the back than the rainbow but shallower in the body. Its flesh is particularly firm and somewhat rubbery, and as such it is a particularly good subject for the smoker as it does not easily suffer damage during handling.

The native brown trout is my favourite fish. It has a distinctive, somewhat 'earthy' flavour, which I find particularly appealing, although more conventional palates might well favour the rainbow. Trout from 225–450 g (8 oz–1 lb) are the best size for smoking.

TROUT PIERCED THROUGH EYES FOR HANGING

Smoking

The fish are gutted, the blood channel removed and the belly cavity well washed under a running tap. Heads are left on as a means of support during processing. The trout should be immersed in 80% brine for 1 hour, and after being taken out should be pierced through the eyes with a thin metal rod, as a convenient method of hanging in the kiln. Small pieces of wood, such as broken matchsticks, should be placed between the lug bones of the fish to keep the belly flaps apart, so that the passage of smoke up the belly is unhindered and the fish is thus able to dry out sufficiently. In the case of a larger fish, it will probably require a second piece of wood lower down the belly.

TROUT PIERCED THROUGH MOUTH AND GILL COVER

The trout should be placed in the kiln while wet with brine, and cold-smoked at 26°C (80°F) until the skins are fairly dry. This is likely to take 6–8 hours in the traditional kiln. The hot-smoking kiln should be pre-heated to 82°C (180°F) and smoke should be flowing freely when the fish are transferred to it. Temperatures will drop until the fish have heated through, and care must then be taken to maintain the heat at a steady 82°C (180°F) for the final hot-smoking period, which takes about 2 hours. If the temperature exceeds 93°C (200°F), there is a grave risk that the heads of the trout will come apart, causing the fish to fall to the bottom of the kiln where they will char. Trout are easy fish to smoke, but this can be a problem.

The final product should have a slightly wrinkled skin, golden in the regions of flank and belly. The flesh should be firm and moist, with a good smoky flavour. Weight loss during smoking is about 15% but, taking into account gut loss, the total weight loss from the fresh, ungutted trout to the finished product could be 25–30%.

SMOKED EEL

The size of the eel to be smoked deserves some consideration, as small eels are hardly worth bothering with, yielding very little final weight of flesh and tending to dry in the process. An eel with a minimum diameter of 4 cm (1½ inches) is required, larger for preference. If live eels are used, they can be killed by stunning them with a blow to the head, then placing them in a container and sprinkling a good quantity of salt over them. This will kill them in about 2 hours and also help to remove a good deal of their natural body slime. The eels are given a good scrubbing to remove more slime and then are gutted, care being taken to make an incision into the flesh, 2.5–4 cm (1–1½ inches) below the vent, in order that the kidney may be removed to prevent tainting. Heads are left on and the eels are brined in 80% brine. Here there is a great diversity of opinion as to how long the eels should be soaked in the brine. Some authorities advocate as little as 10 minutes but for a reasonable-sized eel I would advise 20–30 minutes.

The eels should be pierced with metal rods through the throat from front to back. A few small pieces of wood should

EEL PIERCED THROUGH
THROAT FOR HANGING

A Belly cavity
B Matchsticks to open belly cavity

be inserted along the length of the body cavity to keep the flaps apart and assist in drying and smoke penetration.

Smoking

The eels should be smoke-dried for a period of about 2 hours at 32°C (90°F), then the temperature should be raised to 49°C (120°F) for half an hour; the final period, when the eels are cooked and finished, should be 1 hour at 77°C (170°F). Occasionally, larger eels will require longer at this final temperature, and the weight loss guideline is that the fresh, gutted eel should lose 15–20% of its original weight. Total weight loss from the whole eel to the final smoked product could be in the region of 40%.

Well-smoked eel is a truly gourmet product. It should have a smoky flavour with only a mild taste of salt. The flesh should be white, firm and buttery, but not rubbery, and is excellent with soured cream.

BUCKLING

Traditionally, the buckling is a hot-smoked, whole Baltic herring. It is highly esteemed in all the Scandinavian countries and Germany but is seldom obtainable in the UK, which is a great pity.

Although tradition states that buckling should be prepared from Baltic herring, any good-quality fresh or frozen herring are quite suitable, no matter which sea they swim in.

Smoking

A brine of 70% or 80% should be used and the fish are brined whole for 2–4 hours, with head, guts and milt intact. After brining, the fish should be washed in cold water, then pierced through the eyes with rods, in the same manner as trout. They are hung up to dry for 2–4 hours, depending on the prevailing humidity.

The temperature in the kiln should be 29°C (85°F) when the fish are placed inside. After half an hour the temperature should be slowly raised to 71°C (160°F) and maintained altogether for an hour, giving a kiln-drying period of 1½ hours in all. Some fresh sawdust is now sprinkled on to the glowing embers to provide a dense smoke. The buckling are then finished off at a reduced temperature of 60–70°C (140–158°F) for a period of 1–1½ hours, depending on size. Total weight loss should be 20–25%.

SMOKED MACKEREL

In my opinion, hot-smoked mackerel ranks with the very best of hot-smoked fish products, and the fact that it is relatively cheap to buy is an added advantage. Large numbers of mackerel are taken annually around the shores of Britain, and they can be caught with great ease.

Mackerel quickly lose their character once the initial sea freshness has worn off, so it is most important that very fresh fish are used. A mackerel should at all times feel firm and stiff, like a cucumber. Any hint of flaccidity means that the fish is too far gone for human consumption. Ideally, the mackerel should be in the smoker the same day as it is caught, or the following day at the latest, but of course, if they are gutted and frozen this amounts to the same thing.

Smoking

The mackerel should be gutted and the blood channel removed but the heads left on. They should be brined for 1½–2¾ hours, depending on size, in a 70% or 80% brine. After brining, mackerel should be washed in cold water, as a salt gloss is not required. They should be pierced through the eyes for hanging and small pieces of wood should be placed in the belly cavity to keep the flaps open, as in the case of eels and trout, to ensure correct drying out and smoke penetration. They should be hung to pre-dry for 2 or 3 hours, then placed in the kiln for cold-smoking, which should take 4–6 hours at 26°C (80°F), or until their skins are dry. The temperature in the hot smoker should be raised to 82°C (180°F) and the fish placed inside. Smoke cooking at this temperature varies according to the size of the fish and can take between 2½ and 3½ hours. The appearance of the fish as it cools is an excellent guide. The skin of the belly and flanks should turn a deep golden colour and develop very fine wrinkles, far finer than the wrinkles a smoked trout shows; weight loss should be about 25%. One advantage the smoked mackerel has over some other fish is the ease with which the bones can be removed. After the spine and ribs have been taken out, there is a complete absence of the very fine bones that fish of the herring family seem capable of concealing anywhere.

ARBROATH SMOKIES

The Scottish town of Arbroath is famous for two things: the Declaration of Arbroath, when the king of the Scots and his subjects told the king of England exactly what he could do with himself, and Arbroath smokies. These are manufactured from small haddock or whiting that have had their heads removed and their guts pulled out along with the head, the bellies being left intact. They are tied together in pairs by their tails and can thus be suspended over rods for smoking.

Traditionally, smokies were smoked in barrels set over fires and the final product had a dark, tarry appearance that cannot be achieved in modem mechanical kilns.

Smoking

A 70% or 80% brine is used and the fish are soaked for 30 to 45 minutes. They are a lean fish, so salt penetration is more rapid than is the case with fatty fish such as mackerel and buckling. They should be pre-dried for 2 to 4 hours, then placed in cool smoke (30°C/86°F) for half an hour. The temperature is then raised to 71°C (160°F) and maintained at this heat for a further hour. The fire should then be disturbed and fresh sawdust added to the glowing embers to produce a dense smoke, but the temperature should be dropped to 65°C (150°F) and maintained for 11/2 hours, at the end of which time the smokies are ready. Weight loss should be about 30%.

HOT-SMOKED SALMON

This alternative method of dealing with salmon is becoming better known in the UK. It should in particular commend itself to anyone fortunate enough to catch a fair number of salmon, and who would therefore be most likely to appreciate another method of presenting them. Untraditional as it may be considered, it forms the basis of an excellent salad.

Smoking

The salmon is gutted and the blood channel removed, then beheaded; the lug bones and shoulder plates are removed, as they are not required to hang the fish by. The fish is then cut into segments or steaks, about the size you might expect to find in a large can of tinned salmon. The spinal section is removed from each segment but the skin is left intact. Each piece of fish is washed in cold water, then allowed to drain for 10 minutes. The pieces are now placed in 95% brine (1.5 kg/3 lb 5½ oz salt to 4.54 litres/1 gallon water) for 2 hours, then after removal are washed and drained for 15 minutes. The pieces of salmon are now placed on wire mesh trays and allowed to stand for half an hour at room temperature (18–21°C/65–70°F) with the skin in contact with the tray. Smoking commences at 26°C (80°F) and is gradually raised to 77°C (170°F) over a 3-hour period. This temperature is then maintained and smoking continues for a further period of 2½ hours. The fish is now ready and, as it begins to cool, the skin should be removed.

SMOKED PHEASANTS

The idea that it might be a feasible proposition to smoke pheasants was entirely my own. I am not a fisherman myself but I do shoot and consequently have a fair quantity of game through my hands every season.

We are quite fond of pheasants, but after a time we become tired of them. My wife has managed to purloin a recipe from the daughter of one of the hereditary Scottish clan chiefs, which involves doing a roast pheasant up, off the bone, with cream, garlic and button mushrooms and serving the result on a bed of savoury rice. This alters the character of the bird completely, to such an extent that it is unidentifiable as pheasant, making a welcome change from pheasant done in the conventional manner. We are not keen on keeping pheasants in the freezer

PHEASANT OR CHICKEN IMPALED ON
HAZEL STICK FOR SMOKING

over the summer. There seems to be something not quite right in eating roast pheasants during the close season, so the idea was formulated that it might be possible to smoke pheasants as an alternative.

There is no question as to the success of smoked pheasants, but some care should be exercised over the choice of birds. The young, comparatively fatless birds of October and November are not at all suitable, unless very early hatched and consequently more mature. I would recommend that the pheasants shot during the first couple of months of the season should be utilized in the ordinary manner. Ideally, a pheasant for smoking should be mature with plenty of fat on it. Young birds tend to go dry during the process and are not so full flavoured as the adult birds. An appreciable advantage of smoking pheasants is that old birds can be utilized, as smoking tenderizes elderly game, and the final hot smoking can be slowed down and lengthened until the bird is completely tenderized. A heavy, fat old cock can be ideal – this kind of bird can be difficult to deal with by other methods. Apart from casseroling him in cider or white wine for several hours, he is fit for little else.

The pheasants should be hung in the feather for 3 days before plucking and drawing, and never allowed to become 'high'. They should then be either frozen until required or processed fresh, straightaway.

They should be pricked with a fork in the regions of breast and thighs and covered in brine, weighted down. The brine can either be 90% (1.4 kg/3 lb 1¼ oz per gallon of water) or 80%, prepared as specified for salmon (see pages 69–70). If 90% brine is used, the birds will require soaking for 1¼ hours. They will require 2 hours in the 80% solution.

The birds should be prepared for hanging by fastening a short piece of string to the upper wings, then doing the same with the other end of the string to the opposite wing, thereby forming a loop. The birds should be hung, wet with brine, to drip and pre-dry for 24 hours. They should either be hung in the kiln by their string loops or placed on wire racks, in which case one need not bother to string them. I favour the former course as this allows for the free passage of smoke through the interior of the bird, which should have an opening at the neck end. The pheasants should be cold-smoked for a period of 24 to 48 hours, according to their size and condition. The larger and fatter the birds, the longer I suggest they are given the cold smoke. It does not matter if smoke temperatures in the kiln are low, say 10°C (50°F), but they should not exceed 26°C (80°F). Any birds that appear rather lean will benefit from the application of a painting of olive or vegetable oil over their skins. After cold-smoking, the birds should either be hung in the hot smoker by their string loops or placed on their backs on wire racks.

As pheasants tend to be rather dry-fleshed birds, I believe it is wise to avoid excessively high temperatures during hot smoking.

I regard as ideal 82–88°C (180–190°F) for a period of 3–4 hours, depending on age.

After smoking, the pheasants should be cooled on wire trays and allowed to mature for at least 24 hours before any attempt is made to eat them.

Smoked pheasants are ideal as a meat base for summer salads and make a first-class filling for sandwiches. In fact I can think of nothing better when grouse shooting than sandwiches containing smoked pheasant from the previous season. They have a very delicate taste and highly flavoured additives should be avoided. Horseradish will effectively mask their flavour and

TURKEY, CHICKEN OR PHEASANT STRUNG BY WINGS

should not be used. Only a little lemon juice should be added, or even nothing at all.

SMOKED QUAIL

There are three varieties of quail in Britain. There is the European quail, which occasionally spends the summer and early autumn here, sometimes breeding successfully before migrating back to the Continent before winter sets in. For many years, even before the Protection of Birds Act came into being, the quail has been a completely protected bird in Britain, which is no bad thing considering the persecution it suffers at the hands of our French and Italian neighbours.

Next we have the American bobwhite quail. This is an excellent sporting and eating bird, and is virtually the mainstay of all inland game shooting activities in the USA. They do well in the wild state under favourable climatic and ecological conditions and are fairly easy to rear, so wild stocks can always be augmented should the level of a local population decline for any reason. The bobwhite is a sedentary species and has occasionally bred in the wild in Britain after being released, although our climate is hardly suitable for it to gain a firm enough foothold to become recognized as a resident breeding species.

Lastly we have the Japanese or coturnix quail. To the best of my knowledge, this is not a Japanese wild bird but a commercially manufactured article, created by the Japanese from a foundation of the quail that abounded in millions in the Middle East and many other hot countries in biblical days. The Japanese quail was the original battery hen and was kept in a tiny individual cage with scarcely room to turn round. Under these conditions, a quail would sometimes lay over 365 eggs in the course of a year. The Japanese quail matures at 6 weeks, when it will commence to lay eggs, which will be fertile when the bird is 7 or 8 weeks old.

This quail is the most prolific of the entire, rather extensive quail family, which of course commends it to the commercial producer. As it matures so quickly, it shows an excellent food conversion ratio, probably greater than in any other form of livestock kept for food.

As the Japanese quail is the most readily available, this is the one we must concern ourselves with. In my early days of smoking, smoked quail was not found in many restaurants, and I came across it quite by chance in a hotel in Lancashire. This was at the time when I was playing about with Abu smoke boxes. By trial and error (especially the latter) I produced a more than tolerable product in the Abu, but as I was asked to smoke a fairly large quantity of quail for a commercial establishment I realized that I would need to devise a method of smoking the birds that would deal with them in quantity. Here the situation differed from my own private ventures. The quail I originally dealt with were prime, 6-week-old roasting birds, but my business colleague wanted me to smoke his old ex-laying birds, the bulk of whom were large and fat, some weighing 225–280 g (8–10 oz) dressed, while some were fatless and sinewy, yet all required converting into prime smoked quail.

The method I evolved is as follows. I would prick the quail on either side of the breast to allow the brine to penetrate the flesh more easily. I would soak the birds for an hour, making certain each body cavity was completely filled with brine so that it could penetrate from within also. After brining, I would wash them well and allow to drain on racks for 3 hours. The next stage was an overnight stay in the cold smoker with smoke temperatures at 15–26°C (60–80°F), after which I would stack them in the dustbin-type smoker on wire netting racks on three different levels. The sawdust by this time would be well ignited, and the gas ring placed directly under the bin. The temperature would be raised to 82–93°C (180–200°F) and the birds would cook for 3–4 hours. Invariably, the top rack would turn a deep reddish brown before the lower levels were cooked, so these would be removed and the lower racks moved up a rung, until they, too, were finished in their turn. This worked very well for a time, although I found there was no way to prevent the lower part of the legs going hard and dry.

I was never completely satisfied with this method, or for that matter the rather too elderly merchandise I was handling, which differed from old pheasants in that the latter have sufficient fat and flesh on their bones to prevent their going dry.

However, this commercial contract eventually finished and from there on I was only concerned with my own enterprises, supplying a few birds to hotels and a good many to shooting men who visit our area. I went back to the young roasting birds weighing 112 g (4 oz) or more, and decided on a foolproof technique of processing.

I now brine the birds for an hour but do not prick, as brine can penetrate tender young birds without this assistance. I wash and drain for 3 hours, then give them their 12 hours in smoke at 15–26°C (60–80°F). They are then finished in the Abu. As they have been well smoke-dried already, the Abu burner only requires a single fill of meths to complete the job, taking approximately 20 minutes, provided only two quail are placed in the Abu at any one time. The quail done in this way are superb. They are well smoked and thoroughly cooked, but the final process keeps them very moist and succulent. The smoked quail certainly deserves to be a great deal better known than it is at present, and is one of the best starters one could ever find.

SMOKED GROUSE

I do not feel there is ever any justification for smoking young grouse. Even in the really good grouse years, young grouse are never all that plentiful, compared to the hundreds of thousands of young reared pheasants that are killed and eaten annually. To me, a young grouse remains so much a delicacy in its own right that there is no need to look any further for additional means of presentation than the traditional ways of cooking, as advocated by Mrs Beeton and her successors.

Old grouse are, however, a different matter. Unsuitable for roasting by ordinary methods, they can only be casseroled or made into game pie. I do not decry the grouse served in these particular ways but as there is surely a limit to one's appetite for pies and casseroles, smoking offers a feasible alternative as an outlet for over-yeared birds; in fact, in my opinion, it is the best use to put them to.

Smoking

As I have advocated all along, game for smoking should never be allowed to hang until it goes 'high'. The grouse is certainly no exception to the rule and should be prepared within 2 or 3 days of killing. The birds should be well washed inside after drawing and should be pricked with a fork, twice on either side of the breast, right down to the bone. They should be soaked in

80% brine for 1 hour. Grouse, being lean, fatless birds compared with pheasants and quail, absorb the salt readily so do not require too long in the brine. After brining they should be washed inside and out and then allowed to pre-dry on racks for 6 hours; to prevent the grouse drying up during the smoking process, the birds should be liberally rubbed all over with olive or vegetable oil before being placed in the cold-smoker. I recommend a period of 36 hours at a smoke temperature never exceeding 24°C (75°F) – in fact 15°C (60°F) is better. They can be hung as described in the section on smoked pheasant, with a loop of string attached to their wings, or placed on their backs on wire trays. After cold-smoking, they will require oiling again and the hot-smoker should be allowed to reach a temperature of 82°C (180°F). The birds will require smoke-cooking for a period of 3–3½ hours at this temperature. Higher temperatures are not recommended, as it must at all times be the object of the operator to avoid excessive drying of a naturally dry bird. The finished product is quite an object to behold. Dark mahogany in colour and displaying an attractive oil gloss, it resembles nothing so much as smoked venison. The smoked birds should be left for a day before eating, when it will be possible to slice them wafer thin if desired, as they are firm and close grained in texture and resemble smoked venison in flavour as well as appearance. Only the breasts should be used, as the legs waste away to nothing.

SMOKED DOMESTIC DUCK

Few commodities lend themselves to smoking as well as the domestic duck, provided one is careful at one stage of the process. They are tolerant in the extreme, are very hard to dry up on account of their large amount of natural fat, and are very, very good to eat.

In the past I was very fortunate regarding my raw material, as there lived in the county of Cheshire a very clever livestock breeder. He obtained a nucleus of Japanese quail from a breeder in the north, and within a few generations he had improved the stock by selective breeding and improved feeding techniques so that they were far superior to the birds of his original supplier in shape and flesh-to-bone ratio. He did the same with the ducks. He only kept a pure Aylesbury, without any addition of Pekin blood, which can increase the size but also the fat content of the duck. Unlike some breeders, he retained the keel, or breastbone, in his ducks, whereas some producers have, through either negligence or design, allowed the keel to become almost bred out of their birds. The advantage of the mallard-shaped, keeled ducks is that the depth of this bone allows the bird to develop more muscle, or red meat, on the breasts, so increasing the meat-to-bone ratio of the bird.

I was asked by one purchaser to smoke the largest ducks for him that I could obtain, so for quite a period I operated with ducks weighing 2.25 kg (5 lb) or more. These were quite satisfactory but fat content tends to be high on ducks of this size, and one day my supplier asked me to experiment with some of his 1.8 kg (4 lb) ducks to see how they worked out, as he thought he had an outlet for smoked duck. I decided that a duck of 19 kg (4 lb 5 oz), including giblets, was ideal. There is an initial giblet loss of about 225 g (8 oz), leaving a carcase weight of 1.7 kg (3 lb 13 oz), while a smoking and cooking loss of 310–365 g (11–13 oz) finally provides a smoked duck of approximately 1.34 kg (3 lb).

Smoking

The ducks are well and deeply pricked in the areas of breast, thighs and lower legs, and are immersed in 80% brine. Two and a half hours appears to be about right for the 1.8 kg (4 lb) birds, while birds 450 g (1 lb) heavier will require 3–3½ hours. Their high fat content appears to inhibit salt penetration to a certain degree, but they seem to absorb the salt through the body cavity. After brining, they are strung across the wings and hung up to pre-dry for 24 hours. Now the tricky stage of the process is reached. Unlike many things, ducks cannot be cold-smoked for long periods, yet theoretically, being fat birds and smoke-resistant, they need an appreciable period in smoke. Leave them in too long and they will turn rancid and dangerous to eat. With smoke temperatures of 24–26°C (75–80°F), they should be given exactly 36 hours in the smoke. If ambient temperatures are low and smoke temperatures do not exceed 15°C (60°F), they can be safely smoked for 42 hours. Hot smoking can finally be conducted at temperatures ranging from 82–115°C (180–240°F), the birds requiring 2–5 hours depending on size and temperature. This is the point at which the birds show their tolerance of varying techniques. They should be either suspended on sticks in the dustbin-type smoker (four to a bin) or placed flat on their backs on the shelves of a cabinet-type kiln.

The former method is preferable as the duck can drain as it cooks, whereas when the bird lies on its back, liquid fat forms within the body cavity and is liable to deluge the operator when he or she finally removes it from the kiln, unless great care is taken. Ducks that are suspended by the wings will need their wings pressed back into place while still hot from the smoker, or appearance will suffer. Ducks that have been finished on their backs should ideally be hung up to drain. In any event, ducks are messy creatures to handle on account of their fat content, and should be dried off with paper towelling. Great care must be taken during hot-smoking to ensure that every drop of fat from the birds falls into a drip tin and cannot possibly come into contact with a naked flame. Molten duck fat is highly combustible, igniting with a vivid flash which can in turn ignite the ducks themselves, causing them to burn like roman candles. As I have remarked before, smoking is to a certain extent a process of trial and error, and as far as ducks catching fire goes, I have made my errors.

One of the notable features of all smoked foods, which I have not previously mentioned, is that of aroma. Just as a good wine or a fine brandy has its distinctive bouquet, so should every smoked product have its aroma. The smoked duck has its aroma par excellence and, coupled with its beautiful deep red-gold colour, it makes one of the most attractive as well as one of the most delicious products of the entire smoked range.

SMOKED WOODCOCK

Woodcock are something of a delicacy at any time. They are not normally obtainable in any significant numbers and, roasted on toast in the traditional manner, are appreciated by sportsmen gourmets.

However, I can thoroughly recommend smoked woodcock, and one or two can easily be smoked alongside other species, such as pheasants or quail. When in good condition the woodcock is a fat, moist bird and will retain a good proportion of moisture during smoking.

Smoking

The woodcock should be gutted, as any other bird (the innards are normally left in during other culinary processes). They should be soaked in 80% brine for 1 hour, then allowed to dry on a rack for 3 hours. They are cold-smoked at 21–26°C (70–80°F) for 12–18 hours, then hot-smoked for 2 hours at 93°C (200°F). Alternatively, being small, tender birds, they can be finished off in an Abu smoke box after cold-smoking; the time required for a burner of meths to burn out is sufficient to complete the process.

SMOKED TURKEY

Being large birds, with thick layers of muscle, turkeys do not absorb smoke too readily, but on the other hand are not inclined to go dry during smoking. I have never attempted a very large bird, and I would say turkeys from 2.7–4.5 kg (6–10 lb) dressed weight are ideal. A bird of this size should be deeply pricked with a fork in all fleshy areas to assist brine penetration, then soaked in 80% brine for 4–5 hours, depending on size. The bird should be weighted down to ensure that it is covered in brine at all times, and a convenient method is to place a fairly large stone within the body cavity of the bird. After brining, the turkey should be strung across the wings for hanging and should be allowed to drain for 24 hours. Before being placed in the kiln for cold-smoking, make sure that the bird is well opened at the neck end, so that the smoke can pass freely through the interior of the bird.

Smoking

In order to impart a good smoky flavour to the bird, it is

advisable to give it quite an appreciable period in cold smoke, say 4–7 days at a smoke temperature of 15–26°C (60–80°F). After cold-smoking, it should be hot-smoked for a period for 4–6 hours, depending on the size and age of the bird, at a temperature of 93–104°F (200–220°F). I mention age specifically, as turkey hens that have laid for a season can be a very good buy. They are much cheaper than the young roasting birds and are quite suitable for smoking, provided one gives them an extra couple of hours or so in the hot-smoker.

SMOKED CHICKEN

Much of what I have written about turkeys applies to smoked chicken. Although I have never tried one, I dare say an old boiling fowl could be considerably enhanced by smoking, bearing in mind that it will require a longer hot-smoking period than a young roasting chicken. A 1.8 kg (4 lb) (dressed weight) chicken should be pricked in the same manner as a turkey and soaked in 80% brine for 2½–3 hours.

Smoking

Chickens should be allowed to drain for 24 hours before cold-smoking and should be left in the kiln from 48 hours to 4 days at 15–26°C (60–80°F). A point to be considered in relation to both turkeys and chickens is that, unlike ducks, they will not go rancid during an extended cold-smoking period, so this can be somewhat elastic. They will require about 2 hours' hot-smoking at 104–115°C (220–240°F) to complete the process.

SMOKED VENISON (RED AND ROE)

Red and roe venison can, for all practical purposes, be dealt with together. The treatment is identical, the only differences being in brining and cooking times on account of the differences in size and weight. Only the haunches and saddles are suitable for smoking, as the more frontal areas have not sufficient depth of flesh; in fact the saddle of a roe has only just enough depth of flesh to render smoking a viable proposition.

Venison should have hung for a minimum of 1 week before brining, but on no account should it be allowed to go 'high'. A haunch of roe will require brining for 3 hours in 80% brine, a saddle of roe 2 hours, whereas a haunch of red deer will require 6 hours in the brine and a saddle from the same animal will need 3½ hours in the pickle. I am assuming that the red deer venison will come from ordinary hill beasts, and it is surely a matter of common sense that a haunch from one of those monsters from Thetford Chase would require considerably longer in the brine.

Whether red or roe, haunch or saddle, venison requires pricking well all over to assist brine penetration. After brining, the meat should be allowed to drip for 24 hours. A haunch should be hung by the hock and a saddle should have an incision made in the thin, membraneous flesh between the two ribs which should be included in the saddle when cutting up the beast, and a string loop introduced.

Smoking

Venison is a product that needs to be well smoked to obtain the best results. Roe venison should be cold-smoked for about 7 days at a temperature of 15–24°C (60–75°F). After 3 days it will begin to turn black, which is as things should be. Red venison should smoke from 7 to 10 days, at similar temperatures. After cold-smoking, the femoral artery on the inside of the haunch

HAM OR VENISON HAUNCH SHOWING INJECTION SITES

should be sought and carefully squeezed towards the cut end of the haunch. A small quantity of greenish, rather unpleasant fluid will be squeezed out and should be wiped away with a tissue.

The surface of the venison will now be dry and rather hard, and should be rubbed all over with olive or vegetable oil before being placed in the hot-smoker. It can be placed flat, like a joint of meat, on a rack, and roe venison should be hot-smoked for 2 hours at 104°C (220°F). Red venison will require smoking for 3 hours at this temperature. It is much drier in character than roe and great care must be taken not to overcook, or quality and character will suffer. On no account must smoked venison be eaten until it has aged at least 24 hours. A hard, thin rind will form, which I discard after slicing. The venison above the joint should be carved against the grain towards the bone, the meat below the knee joint being carved downwards along the grain.

Smoked venison is so good that I am delighted to see it is at last becoming popular in this country. For many years it was enjoyed only by Scandinavians, Germans and Dutch in Europe and possibly Red Indians across the Atlantic. Deer stalking in

Scotland is of course traditional, but the sport of woodland stalking is now gaining momentum in very many parts of the country, with roe, Sika and feral fallow as the main quarry. These woodland deer are now becoming regarded as a national asset instead of vermin, and are a valuable addition to the nation's larder.

VENISON (SWEET PICKLE CURED, HOT-SMOKED)

This method is well adapted to dealing with haunches or saddles of venison from a particularly old red deer, whose flesh will probably be very tough and dry.

If desired, the sweet pickle brine can be injected from the brine pump into the thickest parts of the flesh, right down to the bone. The meat is then placed in a crock under refrigeration and allowed to remain in the sweet pickle for a period of 5–7 days for a saddle and 10–14 for a haunch, depending on size. The meat should be turned over every couple of days and the brine should be given a good stir at the same time. After brining, the venison should be washed and allowed to dry under refrigeration for a period of 24 hours for a saddle and 48 hours for a haunch. Opinions vary on how long the meat should be cold-smoked, but it is my own policy never to hurry a smoking process. I recommend that the venison should remain in the cold smoke for 10–14 days, by which time it will have acquired that attractive surface blackening.

In the case of the haunch, the inside of the thigh should be squeezed towards the pelvic bone and the small quantity of greenish fluid from the femoral artery should be wiped away. This substance is probably perfectly harmless, but personally I would rather get rid of it.

Smoking

The venison should be placed in the hot-smoking kiln after its surface has been well oiled and should be smoked at between 93 and 107°C (200 and 225°F) for 2 hours for a saddle and 3 hours for a haunch. I must again stress that you should never attempt to cure and smoke venison that has been dead for less than a week, otherwise it cannot absorb the pickle fully and the flavour will be impaired.

SMOKED CAPERCAILLIE

The traditional Scottish recipe for this, the largest of the British and Scandinavian game birds, states that as soon as possible after the bird has been killed, the crop should be removed, the feet cut off and the bird then buried for a fortnight, by which time one should have forgotten where it has been buried. This implies that the caper is pretty ghastly fare, but this is an exaggeration, and similar defamatory statements are often made about the black grouse and its female counterpart, the grey hen, which I and many others consider excellent eating.

Certainly the crop of the caper should be removed as soon as possible after the bird has been shot. It is most likely to contain conifer sprigs, which can impart a rather resinous flavour to the flesh if not removed. Certainly nothing appears to be gained from the removal of the feet.

In common with all game birds that are to be smoke-cured, the caper should not be allowed to 'hang' for any length of time: 3–4 days is quite sufficient. After plucking and drawing, the caper, being a heavily fleshed bird, should be well pricked in the breast and thighs to let the pickle enter.

A hen bird should be placed in sweet pickle under

refrigeration for 4–5 days. Cocks are considerably larger and will require 6–10 days in the brine, according to size and age.

After brining, the bird should be well washed and allowed to dry off in a refrigerator for 36–48 hours, after which it should be cold-smoked at 21–29°C (70–85°F) for a period of 4–6 days. Hot-smoking should be carried out at 107°C (225°F) for about 21/2 hours if the bird is young, but an old bird is best finished off at 93°C (200°F) for a period of about 4 hours, or even longer if the thigh is still tough when tested with a fork. This process should completely mask any peculiar natural flavour, which the individual might find not to his taste if the bird is simply cooked in the conventional manner.

Old black grouse (blackcocks) can be dealt with in an identical manner. They are tough and can defy conventional cooking methods but smoking will subdue even the oldest.

SMOKED MALLARD, WIGEON, TEAL AND DIVERS

My own preference is for wildfowl to be prepared and cooked according to conventional recipes but all forms of wildfowl can be hot-smoked to great advantage. This is particularly so in the case of wigeon and diving ducks, which are not to every person's taste when cooked in a conventional manner – some consider them to taste fishy. I do not, and enjoy wigeon whether they have been feeding inland or on marine grasses. The divers, pochard and tufted duck do consume small fish but I find these birds perfectly palatable, although I do admit that both wigeon and divers have a very distinctive flavour. Smoking will certainly mask this to a considerable extent.

In common with all feathered game destined for the smoker, wildfowl should be prepared within 3 or 4 days of being shot.

Brining

Fat content of wild ducks varies considerably according to the time of year and on what the birds have been feeding. Basically, wild duck flesh is lean and dark but most ducks carry a layer of subcutaneous fat as insulation against low temperatures. Mallard should be well pricked and brined for about 2–3 hours, depending on fat content, in 80% brine. Teal should be pricked and brined for about 1–1½ hours. Wigeon normally carry less fat than other ducks, relying more on an exceptionally thick layer of blackish down to keep out the cold, so about 1½ hours in the brine suffices. Diving duck usually carry a good layer of fat and require pricking well and brining in 80% brine for about 2–2½ hours.

Smoking

The ducks should be strung by the wings and allowed to drip overnight before being placed in the cold-smoking kiln. Alternatively they can have a meat hook driven through the neck cavity and out between the shoulders, care being taken that the neck cavity remains open to facilitate the free passage of smoke. Teal should be cold-smoked for 12–15 hours at 21–26°C (70–80°F) and mallard for 24 hours. Wigeon and divers will benefit from a longer period in cold smoke, the better to mask their distinctive flavour, say 36–48 hours. Teal can then be treated like quail, and hot-smoked for about 2 hours at 93°C (200°F) but, better still, they can be finished in an Abu. The Abu takes two teal comfortably and one burn of 20 minutes should be sufficient for young teal. If upon examination the birds are underdone owing to their age, another 20-minute burn will finalize the business. Mallard will require 3–3½ hours in the hot-smoker at 88–99°C (190–210°F). Wigeon, being fatless, are best done in the lower temperature ranges, 82–88°C (180–190°F), for from 3–4 hours. Divers, having more fat, can be hot-smoked at 99°C (210°F) for about 3 hours.

Being close-grained, smoked wildfowl can be sliced very thinly and no additives other than a little lemon juice or soured cream should be used.

SMOKED OCTOPUS

Octopus is sometimes served as one of the courses of a gourmet meal, or occasionally as a starter for a less opulent meal. Cooked by ordinary methods it can sometimes be rather tough and tasteless, but it is a seafood that can be enormously improved by smoking. Unlike other seafoods, octopus is rubbery, and in some restaurants tends to remain so after cooking, but the following process will tenderize it.

The body should be cut open and the alimentary tract removed. The octopus should be boiled until a pointed instrument can easily pierce the flesh of the tentacle. The octopus should be allowed to cool and, if it is a large specimen, the dark skin should be removed, as this will be too tough to eat. If the octopus is a small one, say 1.8–2.25 kg (4–5 lb), this dark skin is quite edible. The tentacles should be cut crosswise into slices about 1.2 cm (½ inch) thick. The body should be cut into pieces of comparable size.

The pieces are put in special octopus brine (see page 27) for 1 hour. After removing them from the brine, allow them to drain until dry. They are then placed on oiled wire grids inside the smoker and smoked at a temperature of 54°C (130°F) until they become golden brown.

The octopus is now ready for the table but an interesting variation of the process, for those who prefer a fuller flavour, is to oil the octopus. The smoked sections of octopus are placed in a large glass jar with a screw lid, such as a sweet or pickle jar, and a quantity of olive oil is added. The jar should be rotated end over end until the pieces are all coated in oil. After a short time, the oil will be absorbed, so more oil should be added and the jar rotated again. This process should be repeated until the octopus is saturated in oil and will absorb no more. The oiled octopus is now ready to eat.

Storage

The octopus will keep under refrigeration for several days. Alternatively, it may be bottled in sealed jars.

SMOKED OYSTERS

Fresh, live oysters only must be used. The shells should be well washed to remove any traces of mud or sand and the oysters should then be steamed in a cooker for between 20 and 30 minutes. The meat is then taken out of the now opened shells and soaked in a 50% brine (685 g/1 lb 8½ oz salt per 4.54 litres/1 gallon of water) for 5 minutes. It is a good idea to cut the largest oysters lengthways before brining to assist salt penetration. The oysters should then be placed on wire racks to drain for 15 minutes before placing in the kiln, which should be preheated to 77°C (170°F).

Smoking

The oysters will only require smoking for a total period of 30 minutes and should be turned over half way through the smoking process to give a uniform cure.

SMOKED RAZOR CLAMS

Razor clams should first be steamed for 10 minutes to open them. The meats should be shaken out and the clams cleaned by removing the stomachs and splitting open the necks. They should then be washed and cut into sections. The clams should be soaked in 60% brine (840 g/1 lb 14 oz salt to 4.54 litres/1 gallon of water) for 5 minutes, then rinsed in cold water and drained on racks for 15 minutes.

Smoking

After draining, the meats should be placed on wire racks, oiled with vegetable or olive oil and smoked in very light smoke for 30 minutes at 40°C (105°F). Dense smoke should then be produced and the clams should be smoked for a further 2 hours in this smoke. For the last 30 minutes of the process, smoking should be carried out at a temperature of 77°C (170°F). Weight loss should be 25–30%.

SMOKED PARTRIDGE AND CHUKOR

The grey partridge is a familiar bird in Britain and Europe. Wild ones, however, are only thriving on a few East Anglian estates where the farming is sympathetic. Many are reared on game farms but do not make viable breeders afterwards. They are, however, available as table birds.

The red-legged or French partridge has always remained in a cliff-hanging position in the wild, doing well in some areas yet seemingly incapable of gaining a foothold in other parts, even though helped by man. However, reared red-legs have caught on in a big way recently, and are readily available.

The chukor is a handsome bird, resembling a large French

partridge in appearance. It is an Asiatic and Balkan species, not as yet appearing in the wild state in Britain, but it is bred on one or two game farms purely as a table bird.

All these birds are particularly suitable for smoking and, in common with all game birds to be smoked, they should not be hung until they become 'high' or 'gamy'. The chukor is naturally frozen by the producers, within 24 hours of killing, so can obviously be guaranteed fresh enough for smoking when it is purchased.

My own attitude to young grey partridges is similar to my ideas on young grouse, namely that they are really too much of a rarity in most households to justify any other treatment than conventional cooking methods. However, there is a strong case for smoking the over-yeared birds that one would normally casserole or put in a game pie. My sentiments differ somewhat on the French partridge. The young birds are not so fine-fleshed or delicately flavoured as their grey or 'English' cousins, and can be mass-produced on game farms fairly easily, so I can see nothing against smoking them.

A word on distinguishing old from young partridges is appropriate. The first flight feather on a young grey partridge is V-shaped at the tip. This feather on an old partridge is U-shaped. A young French has a very thin, cream-coloured tip to the first flight feather, about 5 mm (¼ inch) in length. The old bird has no such tip.

Grey or French partridges should be placed in 80% brine for 1¼ hours. The chukor, being a larger bird, requires soaking for 1½ hours. After rinsing in cold water, the birds should be allowed to dry for about 8 hours. Cold-smoking at 21–29°C (70–85°F) should be carried out for 12–18 hours, depending on species, the chukor of course requiring the longer period. The birds will now need oiling with vegetable or olive oil before being transferred to the hot-smoke oven.

For old birds, the smoke oven should be pre-heated to 93°C (200°F) and smoking maintained at this temperature for 2½–3 hours. Young birds should be hot-smoked at 99–107°C (210–225°F) for a period of 1½–2 hours, giving chukor 15 minutes longer.

10 Smoke-roasting

SMOKE-ROASTING

The traditional smoked foods of Britain and Europe are not normally eaten straight from the smoker. In all cases it is usual to allow the food to 'mature' for at least 24 hours after smoking, so that the best possible flavour can be enjoyed. Hot-smoked foods are almost invariably eaten cold, as are some cold-smoked delicacies such as salmon, cod roes and fillets of beef. Others, like kippers, cold-smoked mackerel or finnan haddock, not to mention ordinary smoked bacon, are cooked before eating, but even these products are not used straight from the smoker.

Relatively unknown, then, in Britain and Europe, but common enough in America, are the smoke-roasting processes, in which meat or fowl is seasoned and slow-roast in a smoky atmosphere at temperatures normally from 93–107°C (200–225°F) but never over 121°C (250°F). Higher temperatures are likely to case harden the meat, leaving the interior underdone, so the process must never be hurried by using higher temperatures than those recommended. When smoke-roasting, the oven should always be pre-heated to the required temperature so that the meat begins to cook right away. The smaller the pieces of meat, the quicker they will cook but they will also tend to dry unless care is taken: after seasoning (see below), they should be well coated in olive or vegetable oil, or have pieces of fat bacon laid over them. Any type of hot-smoking oven is suitable for smoke-roasting, but an interesting piece of equipment which is very convenient and easy to use is the wheelbarrow smoker.

A steel wheelbarrow should have a 10 cm (4 inch) layer of sand or small stones put in the bottom. An oven grid is supported by bricks or concrete blocks, to stand about 30 cm (1 foot) above the bed of sand; better still is a specially constructed barbecue grid standing on its own legs. A charcoal fire is lit under the grid, and, when it is glowing well, sawdust is placed at one end of the coals to provide smoke, but not in such quantity that the charcoal is covered and therefore unable to give off sufficient heat to cook the meat. The fish or meat, well oiled, should be laid on the grid, and a sheet of aluminium foil formed into a cone-shaped cover, which is then fitted around the grid to cover the food. A few holes should be made near the point of the cone to allow steam and smoke to escape.

According to wind and weather conditions, it may be necessary to build a shield of tin or bricks around the grid to conserve the heat and to prevent the smoke being blown away by a strong wind. Half way through the cooking process, the cone should be temporarily removed and the meat or fish turned to ensure even cooking.

Basic seasoning for smoke-roast meat
1.5 kg (3½ lb) salt
8 tablespoons white sugar
2 tablespoons onion salt
4 tablespoons celery salt

2 tablespoons garlic salt

4 tablespoons paprika

8 tablespoons black pepper

8 tablespoons white pepper

4 tablespoons crushed dill

STEAKS

Four cuts of steak are normally used for quick cooking: rump, sirloin, fillet and T-bone. The latter, as the name implies, is left on the bone, and in effect is simply a cross-section cut from a piece of sirloin on the bone but with the flap or 'skirt' piece removed, as this is too tough for quick cooking.

Fillet is very tender, even when it comes from sub-standard animals, and cooks very quickly. Rump is the most solid-textured of all, and must come from a young animal if it is to cook reasonably quickly. Cooking times for sirloin or T-bone steaks fall some way between those for rump and fillet. They should be rubbed well with basic seasoning half an hour before cooking, then have oil applied immediately before being placed in a smoke oven pre-heated to 93–107°C (200–225°F) or on the wheelbarrow grid. Fifteen to 30 minutes is usually sufficient, depending on the cut of steak.

SPARERIBS

Spareribs should be cold-smoked for 12 hours before cooking. Bacon spareribs are already salted and cured, but pork spareribs should be soaked in 80% brine for 30 minutes, air-dried for 12 hours, then smoked. Alternatively, they can be well rubbed with basic seasoning instead of being brined. A large batch of spareribs can be cold-smoked and then frozen for future use.

The spareribs should be smoke-roasted at 121°C (250°F) until crisp, and should be turned occasionally.

HAMBURGERS

Equal quantities of good-quality beef and pork should be minced and bound with egg yolk and basic seasoning to form cakes. These should be placed on a wire rack, with a dripping tin underneath, in a smoke oven pre-heated to 93–107°C (200–225°F). There should be plenty of dense smoke as the hamburgers will only be in the oven for about 30 minutes. They can either be left in the same position for the whole process or can be turned half way through.

CURED BEEF

Good-quality lean beef should be used. Topside or leg steak is ideal, being solid-textured but flavoursome. The beef should be cured in sweet pickle at 1.5°C (35°F). For pieces weighing about 900 g (2 lb), cure for 3–5 days. Cuts of 3–3.58 kg (7–8 lb) will require 10–14 days in the pickle. Before pickling it is essential that the beef should have been dead for a minimum of 7 days, otherwise the fibres will not absorb the pickle properly. After curing, the meat should be washed in cold water and left to dry under refrigeration for 24 hours. Rub well with basic seasoning.

The beef will now require cold-smoking for a period of 12–24 hours at a temperature of 24–29°C (75–85°F), then the process should be completed in the smoke oven, pre-heated and maintained at 93°C (200°F), certainly no higher than 107°C (225°F). Close-textured beef such as topside and leg steak requires slow cooking for the best results. Cooking times will vary from 2 to 4 hours, depending on the size of the cut.

Beef processed as described has a shelf life under ordinary refrigeration of at least a month and can easily be frozen for much longer periods. If this is done, the beef should first be cut up into suitably sized pieces, so that it can later be used as required.

BILTONG

Real biltong, as produced in South Africa, consists of narrow strips of meat, salted and sun-dried. The flesh of game animals is used, also ostrich, and the most highly esteemed and expensive is springbok biltong. Britain does not have a climate that is consistently dry and sunny enough to allow for the production of biltong by traditional methods, but it is possible to produce an excellent smoked substitute. Good cuts of beef or venison should be used, and I imagine goat's flesh would be ideal, being closely related to the antelope family. I have tried the flank and rib flesh of fallow deer but, though the flavour was good, the flesh was too fibrous to swallow.

All fat should be trimmed off, as although the finished product will keep for a long time without refrigeration, fat will turn rancid. The meat should be cut into strips 2.5–4 cm (1–1½ inches) thick. The strips of meat are now cured in sweet pickle brine for 5–7 days. The meat is rinsed in fresh water and dried under refrigeration for 24 hours. The strips of meat are next cut into very thin slices with a very sharp knife. This will be easier if the meat is placed in the freezer until partly frozen – this will make it much firmer during slicing. Cured meat seasoning should be applied to both sides of the slices as an additional flavouring only, as the period the meat has remained in the brine will have been enough to cure it.

The meat slices can have pieces of string passed through holes made in their ends, for hanging in the smoker, or can be laid flat on racks. Cold-smoking takes place at a temperature of 10–29°C (50–85°F) – actually the lower the better. According to smoke temperature and atmospheric humidity, smoking time can vary between 24 hours and 4 days. When a slice will snap in two when it is bent, the meat is ready.

There is no need to freeze the finished product, which will keep almost indefinitely when stored in a container with perforated sides or lid to allow for the free circulation of air.

SMOKED RABBIT PIE

For this rather unusual dish you will require:

> 1 full-sized rabbit
> 335 g (12 oz) belly pork
> 2 medium-sized onions, sliced
> 225 g (8 oz) mushrooms
> 4 eggs, smoked (see page 85) and cut into pieces
> Salt
> Pepper
> Shortcrust pastry

Ideally, the rabbit should have been dead just 3 days, and have hung at normal room temperature or been kept in a refrigerator in hot weather. After skinning, the rabbit should be well washed and soaked in salt water for 3 hours. Then it should be pricked with a fork in the thickest parts of the flesh. The carcase, along with the belly pork, should be placed in 90% brine.

Rabbit and belly pork should be cold-smoked for 24 hours at 24–32°C (75–90°F) and should not be pre-dried before smoking commences. The rabbit is then cut into joints and placed in a casserole along with the sliced belly pork and the onions. The mushrooms are now added, the contents of the casserole just covered with water, and salt and pepper sprinkled over the surface. The casserole is placed in the oven for 1½–3 hours, according to the age of the rabbit, at a temperature of 175°C (350°F/Gas Mark 4). Alternatively, the meat, mushrooms and onions can be cooked in a pressure cooker until tender. The meat should be allowed to cool just enough so that the flesh can be removed from the bones. The rabbit meat, belly pork, mushrooms and onions are now placed in a pie dish with the smoked eggs. The dish is covered with a sheet of shortcrust pastry in which a few holes are made to allow steam to escape. The pie is baked at 220°C (425°F/Gas Mark 7) for 20 minutes. It is equally good eaten hot or cold.

11 Storage of
smoked food

I have already remarked that, owing to modern refrigeration techniques, it is no longer necessary to smoke food as a means of preservation. Many smoked foods will keep for at least 3 weeks under ordinary refrigeration, and most will retain their quality for some months when frozen, if protected adequately against 'freezer burn'. Ordinary polythene wrapping offers no such protection but aluminium foil does and, oddly enough, so does brown paper. When food is wrapped in aluminium foil, the foil should be squeezed around it so that it becomes moulded to fit the contours. Offering better protection still is a heavy-duty opaque polythene wrapping, which is used in conjunction with a vacuum-packing technique in modern poultry-producing establishments. The majority of such establishments will, at a small cost, vacuum-pack smoked fowl, from quail to turkeys and various smoked meats, for the home smoker. A vacuum-packer for domestic use, which cuts and seals polythene bags to size, is also available (see page 142).

Frozen smoked food thaws out fairly rapidly. Freezing turns the fluid that is trapped in the tissues of fish, flesh or fowl to ice. The more ice that is formed, the longer it will take for the food to thaw out again. Smoking removes a good deal of this moisture, and so the smoked article thaws out quicker than the raw material. All products should be eaten within 24 hours of thawing.

12 Commercial production

The home smoker and his or her family will have greatly enjoyed the results of their excursions into this fascinating art. So will their friends, who pronounce their smoked salmon, trout and eels to be vastly superior to anything they have tasted in the most exclusive restaurants. The rarer delicacies they will have tasted for the first time, and have no doubt expressed amazement that such fine fare is not readily available in better-class delicatessens.

Small wonder, then, that the home smoker may be encouraged to consider smoking on a grander scale, but you would be well advised to take several factors into account before embarking on any large-scale ventures.

Certain smoked foods are traditional and are widely accepted. Smoked salmon, trout, kippers, finnans, cod and haddock fillets and Arbroath smokies are all well known in the UK and the demand for these commodities is steady. Several large-scale processing plants are already in operation and seem to work quite profitably. This, however, makes the production of these particular foods highly competitive, and the expanding home smoker might well find it difficult to compete with the larger concerns on price. Your products might be considerably superior to the larger company's, dependent as it is on paid (and frequently disinterested) labour and more hurried processes in the interests of economy, but you will not be able to use the vast quantities of raw material that the larger company is able to process, so you are unlikely to be able to buy at the same favourable rate and consequently will be unable to sell your finished products as cheaply as the established large concern.

What, then, of your specialities, which you alone produce and your larger rivals have probably never even heard of? Although smoked foods are a traditional part of the British culinary heritage, I find that the British are quite conservative when it comes to trying new ones – or at least are unlikely to buy them on a regular basis. Non-shooting people in Scandinavia and Germany appear to have a far greater appreciation of game, both smoked and fresh, than do their counterparts in the UK.

Another difficulty is lack of continuity. Smoked delicacies can never be cheap, if the producer is to make a decent profit, so it is quite common for customers to make a purchase, be absolutely delighted with it, but to feel they cannot afford it again for some considerable time. Doubtless they tell their friends, who say, 'Marvellous, we must try some', then promptly forget all about it.

I know that several small smoking concerns have come into being, quickly gained a good reputation, then faded out through lack of patronage. It is, therefore, my advice to any home smoker not to attempt to 'go commercial' exclusively. If you can do some commercial smoking as a sideline, well and good. It will prove a profitable extension to a fascinating hobby and should slowly help to educate the public into trying and enjoying some of the rarer specialities.

If you live in a rural area, help may be obtained under various funding schemes, such as DEFRA's Rural Enterprise Scheme or their Process and Marketing scheme, which can assist with building and equipment costs. Additional information can be obtained from your regional office of DEFRA (Department for the Environment, Food and Rural Affairs).

Of course a licence for the production of food for sale must be obtained from the local council, but will present no problem if the grant-aided scheme is utilized and the premises brought up to the required standard. So I would encourage home smokers to 'have a go' part-time, but would do my utmost to discourage them from burning their boats and attempting to make a full-time living from this type of work.

1

SUMMARY OF SMOKING DOS AND DON'TS

1 Change brine regularly and keep brining tubs clean.

2 Only use top-quality fresh fish.

3 Always remove the blood channel from fish.

4 Always remove the kidney from eels.

5 Do not hang winged game for more than 3 days before brining.

6 Beef and venison must age for a minimum of 1 week before brining.

7 Do not use wet fuels for smoking. It can give a mouldy flavour to the product and will hinder drying. If only wet sawdust is available, it should be spread thinly on a clean floor to dry.

8 Do not use resinous woods or a bitter flavour will be given to the product.

9 Do not leave ducklings in cold smoke for more than 36 hours or they may turn rancid.

10 When hot-smoking fish, never allow the smoke temperature to exceed 88°C (190°F) or the fish will disintegrate. Try to keep it at 82°C (180°F).

11 Leave all products in brine for the full specified time.

12 Maintain fish at a chill temperature (0°C/32°F) while awaiting processing.

13 Use only good-quality solid salt with no magnesium additives.

14 Hang fish to dry after brining for specified times to allow them to develop a good surface salt gloss.

15 Maintain smoking units and racks in clean condition.

16 Do not allow ash to accumulate.

17 Smoking should be carried out for full recommended times, at correct temperatures.

18 Always allow the product to cool completely before either packaging or freezing.

19 Do not eat any smoked product until it has aged for at least 24 hours. If eaten before 24 hours, no harm will result but the full flavour will not have developed.

20 Do not smoke very young pheasants.

21 Remember to 'feed' the cut surface of frozen salmon with oil before placing in the smoker.

22 Do not smoke young grouse – they are better roasted.

23 Salmon under 3.58 kg (8 lb) should be split rather than filleted.

24 Do not overcook venison, particularly red.

25 Always ensure that salmon loses 17% of its weight during smoking.

26 Do not let your ducks catch fire.

27 When brining poultry and winged game, make certain the body cavity of the bird is completely filled with brine.

28 If the gas flame should blow out during hot-smoking, remove the hot-smoker from the gas ring in the case of a bin or barrel smoker. If a cabinet smoker is involved, give plenty of time for escaped gas to clear, as, if the gas ring is re-lit too soon, gas that has lodged will explode, possibly burning you and the product.

29 Solid fuels, such as small logs, can be used for smoke production, but the fire needs attention. It has to be replenished regularly and care must be taken that it does not blaze up and exceed the desired temperatures, in which case damping down with sand may be necessary. Sawdust, on the other hand, burns with a steady heat at low temperatures, and requires little attention.

2
BRINE STRENGTHS AT 15°C (60°F)

Salt per 4.54 litres (1 gallon) water

10%	125 g (4½ oz)	70%	1.01 kg (2 lb 4¼ oz)
20%	250 g (9 oz)	75%	1.1 kg (2 lb 7½ oz)
30%	385 g (13¾ oz)	80%	1.2 kg (2 lb 10¾ oz)
40%	535 g (1 lb 3 oz)	85%	1.3 kg (2 lb 14¼ oz)
50%	685 g (1 lb 8½ oz)	90%	1.4 kg (3 lb 1¾ oz)
55%	760 g (1 lb 11 oz)	95%	1.5 kg (3 lb 5½ oz)
60%	840 g (1 lb 14 oz)	100%	1.6 kg (3 lb 9½ oz)
65%	925 g (2 lb 1 oz)		

3
STORAGE LIFE OF CERTAIN SPECIES OF SMOKED FISH

		15°C (60°F)		0°C (32°F)	
		In top condition	Edible	In top condition	Edible
		Days	Days	Days	Days
Species	Finnans	2–3	4–6	4–6	8–10
Haddock	Finnans (straws)	1–2	2½–3	4	6–7
	Smokies				
	(hot-smoked)	1–2	2½–3	3–4	5–6
Herring	Kippers	2–3	5–6	4–6	10–14
	Buckling				
	(hot-smoked)	1–2	2–3	3–4	5–6
Salmon	Fillets and split fish				
	(cold-smoked)	3–4	5–6	5	11
Trout	Whole (hot-smoked)	3	7	6	10

Some of the keeping times given may not seem very long for well-cured products, but allow for a good margin of safety healthwise.

4
STORAGE LIFE OF GENERAL TYPES OF SMOKED FISH IN FREEZER CONDITIONS

Type of Fish

	Smoked white fish *	Smoked fatty fish * *
At −9°C (15°F)		
Good	1 month	3 weeks
Inedible	3 months	2 months
At −20°C (−5°F)		
Good	3½ months	2 months
Inedible	10 months	5 months
At −34°C (−29°F)		
Good	7 months	Over 1 year
Inedible	4½ months	Over 9 months

* Finnans, cod and haddock fillets
* * Salmon, mackerel, kippers, eels, buckling

5
RELATIVE HUMIDITY OF THE ATMOSPHERE IN RELATION TO SMOKE CURING

Notes on measurement

Two ordinary mercury-in-glass thermometers are required with a range of about 10–38°C (50–100°F). They must be inserted through holes in the wall of the kiln a few inches apart so that the bulbs project well into the smoke stream. One of the thermometers (the 'wet bulb') has a muslin bag or sleeve tied round the bottom inch or two of the stem, so that it completely surrounds the mercury bulb.

Before a reading is taken, this bag is moistened by dipping in clean water, preferably distilled water, and after putting back in position, the reading of the thermometer is taken when it is steady after about half a minute. The ordinary temperature of the dry bulb should be read on the other thermometer at the same time as that of the wet bulb. The smoke should not pass over the wet bulb immediately before the dry bulb in case the air gets cooled by evaporation before affecting the dry bulb.

From the two readings, the relative humidity of the air or smoke expressed in percentage of saturation with moisture vapour at the dry bulb temperature is obtained using the table of figures given below.

The temperature of the wet bulb is normally lower than that of the dry bulb, because, as the water on the muslin sleeve dries, it cools the mercury bulb and lowers the temperature read on the scale. The drier the air, the greater the 'wet bulb depression', i. e. the dry bulb temperature minus the wet bulb temperature.

If the air is completely saturated with moisture vapour, i. e. the relative humidity is 100%, no further evaporation can take place, the wet sleeve cannot dry and thus the wet bulb reading is the same as that of the dry bulb.

While the flavours are mostly due to the smoke and the initial salting treatments, the flesh texture is largely dependent on the drying process. The amount of drying to which the product has been subjected before smoking will, of course, also affect the final product texture.

Efficient drying processes depend on the humidity of the surrounding atmosphere. The degree of saturation of the air with water vapour is termed the relative humidity (RH). Air which is completely saturated is at 100% RH, and air containing half as much water vapour as it can hold at any temperature is said to be at 50% RH. The best range of relative humidity for cold-smoking purposes, where temperatures of 29°C (85°F) are used, is between 60 and 70%.

Dry bulb, °F	Difference between dry and wet bulb temperatures, °F																			
	1	2	3	4	5	6	7	8	9	10	11	12	13	14	15	16	17	18	19	20
70	95	90	86	81	77	72	68	64	59	55	51	48	44	40	36	33	29	25	22	19
71	95	90	86	81	77	72	68	64	60	56	52	48	45	41	37	33	30	27	23	20
72	91	90	86	82	77	73	69	65	61	57	53	49	45	42	38	34	31	28	24	21
74	95	91	86	82	78	74	69	65	61	58	54	50	47	43	39	36	33	29	26	23
75	96	91	86	82	78	74	70	66	62	58	54	51	47	44	40	37	34	30	27	24
76	96	91	87	82	78	74	70	66	62	59	55	51	48	44	41	38	34	31	28	25
77	96	91	87	83	79	74	71	67	63	59	56	52	48	45	42	39	35	32	29	26
78	96	91	87	83	79	75	71	67	63	60	56	53	49	46	43	39	36	33	30	27
79	96	91	87	83	79	75	71	68	64	60	57	53	50	46	43	40	37	34	31	28
80	96	91	87	83	79	75	72	68	64	61	57	54	50	47	44	41	38	35	32	29
81	96	92	88	84	80	76	72	68	65	61	58	55	51	48	45	42	39	36	33	30
82	96	92	88	84	80	76	72	69	65	61	58	55	51	48	45	42	39	36	33	30
83	96	92	88	84	80	76	73	69	66	62	59	56	52	49	46	43	40	37	34	32
84	96	92	88	84	80	76	73	69	66	62	59	56	52	49	46	43	40	37	35	32
85	96	92	88	84	80	77	73	70	66	63	60	57	53	50	47	44	41	39	36	33
86	96	92	88	84	81	77	73	70	66	63	60	57	53	40	47	44	42	39	36	33
87	96	93	88	85	81	77	74	70	67	64	61	57	54	51	48	46	43	40	37	34
88	96	92	88	85	81	77	74	70	67	64	61	57	54	51	48	46	43	40	37	35
89	96	92	89	85	81	78	74	71	68	65	61	58	55	52	49	47	44	41	39	36
95	96	93	89	86	82	79	76	73	69	66	63	61	58	55	52	49	47	44	42	39
96	96	93	89	86	82	79	76	73	69	66	63	61	58	55	52	50	47	44	42	39
97	96	93	89	86	83	79	76	73	70	67	64	61	58	56	53	50	48	45	43	40
98	96	93	89	86	83	79	76	73	70	67	64	61	58	56	53	50	48	45	43	40
99	96	93	89	86	83	80	77	73	70	67	64	62	59	56	55	51	49	46	44	41
100	96	93	89	86	83	80	77	73	70	68	65	62	59	56	54	51	49	46	44	41

Percentage relative humidities of air from readings of temperatures of wet and dry bulb thermometers. This table is from the original edition and is not converted into °C as we feel it is more useful in this form.

Where RH is above 70% the drying process is too slow, and if below 60% the fish surface dries too quickly.

In other words, the air and smoke draught speed and their capacity to dry products depends on how much the air entering the smoke unit is warmed by the fire. Where cool, dry air enters and is warmed, it will be much lighter than the air outside and will thus travel rapidly up the smoke unit and over the product. The quantity of water vapour that this air will absorb depends on its temperatures, so that if the cool dry air is warmed on entering the smoke unit, its drying capacity will be considerably increased. Where humid ambient conditions exist, the already warm, saturated air cannot be further warmed quickly enough to reduce the water vapour content and thus its capacity for drying the product is reduced.

Thus in the first stage of any smoking process, moisture is removed at a rate dependent on the drying capacity of the air and smoke and their speed over the product. During the second stage of the process, when the surface has dried somewhat, its temperature gets closer to that of the air and smoke. The rate of drying becomes slower, however, as moisture has now got to move out from the inner layers of the flesh. If the initial drying stage is carried out at too high a temperature, too quickly, the result will be to harden the fish surface, making it difficult to remove inner moisture. In this instance there may be no drying effect at the centre of the product.

In hot smoking, the product must not at first be subjected to the higher temperatures involved. The process should start at a relatively low temperature to enable the product to dry partially and the skin to harden. Only then should the heat be increased to cook and smoke the product. Where too high a temperature is reached in the early stage of the process, the product cooks quickly, and as it is still soft and moist, it will break and fall into the fire.

When smoking fatty fish, the initial drying period can be reduced, using a slightly higher temperature, as the presence of some oil prevents hardening of the surface. However, the oil also retards the movement of moisture from below the flesh surface and thus the overall time of the drying process becomes longer.

As spoilage bacteria are more active in moisture-laden products, the drying process is very important. The keeping time of the product will depend, to a large extent, on the amount of moisture removed. Products that have been lightly smoke cured will spoil almost as fast as the raw material from which they were made. Products that have been very heavily cured may keep for many months at normal temperature.

Food will, of course, lose weight during the drying process as the water content is evaporated, and cold-smoke cures with a weight loss of 12–18% on drying will result in good-quality products. Cooked products, obtained when hot smoked, will generally lose considerably more weight than this. The length of the drying process will depend, to a great extent, on the experience of the smoker regarding a particular smoke cure, and will involve consideration of such factors as flesh texture, prevailing weather conditions and whether cold or hot smoking is involved.

USEFUL ADDRESSES

Smokers and other equipment

Afos Ltd
Unit 5
Kingswood Business Park
Connaught Road
Kingswood
Hull
HU7 3AP
Tel: 01482 372100;
fax: 01482 372150
www.afosfood.com
Supplies Torry Kilns.

Gerry's of Wimbledon
170 The Broadway
London
SW19 1RX
Tel: 020 8542 7792
Will supply the Abu Smoke Box by mail order.

Nisbets
1110 Aztec West
Bristol
BS32 4HR
Tel: 01454 855551;
fax: 01454 855565
www.nisbets.co.uk
Suppliers of professional and domestic catering equipment. Stocks the Brookes Super Hot Smoker Unit, plus a cold-smoke attachment.

Pifco Ltd
Princess Street
Failsworth
Manchester
M35 0HS
Tel: 0161 947 3000
Produces a bag sealer that vacuum-packs foods ready for freezing. Contact for details of your nearest stockist.

Stamford Smokers
Terracotta House
First Drift
Wothorpe
Stamford
Lincolnshire
PE9 3JL
Tel/fax: 01780
756563
*Sells an American
water smoker, which
can also be used as a
conventional dry
smoker.*

West Country Stoves
21 Creedy Road
Crediton
Devon
EX17 1EW
Tel/fax: 01363
773557
www.coldsmoker.com
*Sells a dedicated cold
smoker, plus fish
filleting and gutting
knives.*

Ingredients

Angus Quality Meats
Low Wool Oaks
Calthwaite
Penrith
Cumbria
CA11 9RZ
Tel/fax: 01768
885384
www.countryfarms.c
o.uk
*Sells its own well-hung
Aberdeen Angus beef.*

The Game Larder
24 The Parade
Claygate
Surrey
KT10 0NU
Tel: 01372 462879
*Supplies game by mail
order, including
pheasant, venison,
duck, wild boar, grey
and red-legged
partridge.*

The Natural Casing
Company Ltd
PO Box 133
Farnham
Surrey
GU10 5HT
Tel: 01252 850454;
fax: 01252 851284
*Supplies natural
casings for making
sausages at home. Also
stocks saltpetre.*

Wild Beef
Hillhead Farm
Chagford
Devon
TQ13 8DY
Tel/fax: 01647
433433
*Cattle are slaughtered
locally and hung for
four weeks.*

Yorkshire Game Ltd
18 Leaside
Newton Aycliffe
County Durham
DL5 6DE
Tel: 01325 316320;
fax: 01325 320634
www.yorkshiregame.
co.uk
*Supplies boxes of
venison, game birds,
rabbit and wood
pigeon.*

Other useful addresses

British Association
for Shooting and
Conservation
Marford Mill
Chester Road
Rossett
Wrexham
Clwyd
LL12 0HL
Tel: 01244 573000;
fax: 01244 573001
www.basc.org.uk
*Promotes the
development of
country shooting.*

www.wheretofish.com
*Website listing
thousands of fishing
locations, plus a list of
fishing clubs and
associations in
England.*

DEFRA Helpline
17 Smith Square
London
SW1 3JR
Tel: 08459 335577;
fax: 020 7238 3329
www.defra.gov.uk
*Contact the DEFRA
Helpline for
information on
funding schemes if
you are thinking of
starting commercial
production of smoked
foods.*

INDEX